IDIOT'S GUIDES.

AS EASY AS IT GETS!

Pressure Cooking

by Tom Hirschfeld

ALPHA

A member of Penguin Random House LLC

Publisher: Mike Sanders
Associate Publisher: Billy Fields
Managing Editor: Lori Cates Hand
Cover and Book Designer: Becky Batchelor
Compositor: Ayanna Lacey
Proofreader: Catherine Schwenk
Indexer: Brad Herriman

First American Edition, 2015
Published in the United States by DK Publishing
6081 E. 82nd Street, Indianapolis, Indiana 46250

A Penguin Random House Company

15 16 17 18   10 9 8 7 6 5 4 3 2 1

001-289069-April2016

Published in the United States by Dorling Kindersley Limited.

ISBN: 978-1-61564-888-7

Library of Congress Catalog Card Number: 2015948633

Note: This publication contains the opinions and ideas of its author(s). It is intended to
provide helpful and informative material on the subject matter covered. It is sold with
the understanding that the author(s) and publisher are not engaged in rendering
professional services in the book. If the reader requires personal assistance or
advice, a competent professional should be consulted. The author(s) and publisher
specifically disclaim any responsibility for any liability, loss, or risk, personal or
otherwise, which is incurred as a consequence, directly or indirectly, of the use and
application of any of the contents of this book.

DK books are available at special discounts when purchased in bulk for sales
promotions, premiums, fund-raising, or educational use. For details, contact:
DK Publishing Special Markets, 345 Hudson Street, New York, New York 10014
or SpecialSales@dk.com.

Printed in China

idiotsguides.com

Contents

meaty main dishes **131**

Introduction

During the 6 months it took me to write this book, I cooked almost exclusively with pressure cookers. Previously, I had used my pressure cooker on a fairly regular basis, but far from daily. Now that the book is just about finished, I wonder if I can go back to "traditional" cooking. At the same time I have to ask myself, *Why would I?*

A pressure cooker can cook almost anything. It handles some ingredients better than others, but the array of foods that cook better under pressure is amazing. I'll never again cook a pork loin in anything but a pressure cooker. Custards and cheesecake will be baked under pressure from here on out. Rice? Never again in a rice cooker, when the texture of pressure cooked grains is superior. And in the pressure cooker, old-fashioned southern cornbread develops a wonderful crumb and stays so moist. Pressure cookers also are efficient. They require less energy than traditional cooking methods, and they take about a third the time necessary for other methods. And despite the general fear of pressure cookers over the years, they're actually quite safe. Thanks to advances in safety, technology, and precision manufacturing, modern pressure cookers are virtually foolproof. With multiple valves to release pressure and the knowledge that the rubber gasket is meant to release steam if pressure becomes too high, you can set aside your worries.

Full of fresh, whole food ingredients, the recipes in this book are a compilation of classic American comfort foods and international classics, from beef brisket to Caribbean curried chicken to French crème brûlée. There's lots to choose from—and to keep you from ever becoming bored with making dinner again. You can use either a traditional stovetop pressure cooker or a more modern electric pressure cooker, and instructions for both are given in each recipe. Cooking times, temperatures, and techniques can differ by type of cooker, so be sure to read and follow the recipe closely, understanding that times may vary. The user's manual for your specific cooker is a good reference, so familiarize yourself with it if you haven't already. And note that the cook time in all the recipes is the pressure cook time. Any other cooking called for is incorporated in the prep time. A pressure level is also called out so you can see at a glance what level you need to achieve.

Acknowledgments

I have to say thanks to all those who put up with my incessant talk about how amazing pressure cooking is, about my discoveries each day, and why they should buy a pressure cooker. But most importantly, I say thanks to my wife, Amy, and my daughters, Vivian and Lynnie, who were my taste-testers and had very strong opinions about which recipes were best and should be included in the book. To my father, thanks for watching the girls so I could work, and to my mother, thanks for being a good cook yourself. Lastly, thanks to all those in the food industry, chefs, line cooks, servers, and dishwashers, who do a thankless job day in and day out, so that when I don't feel like cooking, I don't have to.

Special Thanks to the Technical Reviewer

Idiot's Guides: Pressure Cooking was reviewed by an expert who double-checked the accuracy of what's presented here to help us ensure making mouthwatering meals in your pressure cooker is as easy as it gets. Special thanks are extended to Joseph Ewing, RD, LDN.

pressure cooker
basics

How Pressure Cooking **Works**

Versatile, easy-to-use pressure cookers enable you to create fresh, whole-food dishes quickly. Pressure cooking isn't a shortcut but rather a time- and energy-efficient cooking method that produces nutritious, delicious dishes.

Faster Cooking

It doesn't matter whether you use a traditional stovetop pressure cooker or a more modern electric version—the science is the same. Rather than boiling food, a pressure cooker uses pressurized heat to cook. Liquid under pressure becomes hotter than normal; as the pressure inside the cooker rises, the temperature of the liquid rises, too—up to 250°F (120°C). A pressure cooker is similar to a steam oven, but because a cooker heats at the same temperature on all sides, it cooks foods very evenly—and in about a third of the time of traditional cooking methods!

Safer Than Ever

Scientifically, pressure cookers work the same as they always have, but technologically, today's cookers are safer than ever. Thanks to the creation of spring-loaded pressure valves and precision manufacturing methods, the days of lids screwed down with bolts and clogged steam valves are no more. At the end of the day, however, a pressure cooker still uses valves to regulate the pressure and temperature.

THE HANDLES
Your pressure cooker might have one or two handles. These can get hot, so test them first and use an oven mitt or a dry, folded kitchen towel if they're too hot. If the handles ever become loose, you can usually tighten them using a screwdriver.

Browning food in a pressure cooker before adding liquids and locking on the lid creates deeper, richer flavor in your finished dish. This is thanks to the Maillard reaction, a chemical reaction between amino acids and sugars that creates intensified flavors. The Maillard reaction really takes off at 250°F (120°C) and higher, so it occurs when a pressure cooker is at a pressure of 15 pounds per square inch (PSI), which is level 2 for traditional pressure cookers and high for electric cookers.

THE LID

The lid is where the magic happens. The lid houses the pressure valves, the rubber seal gasket, and the locking mechanism.

THE POT

A pressure cooker pot is similar to other pots and pans, with the exception of the lip at the top, which has tabs to lock the lid in place. Be careful not to let gas burner flames come up the sides of the pot; keep them within the diameter of the heat-conducting bottom plate so the sides don't become overly hot and scorch the food (or worse, warp the pot).

THE BOTTOM

Good pressure cookers have a thick, heat-conducting plate on the bottom that evenly disperses heat, allows you to maintain the temperature while lowering the heat, and helps prevent scorching.

What Your **Pressure Cooker** Can Do

Pressure cookers can do more than just one-pot meals. These multifunctional cookers are really quite versatile. Want a pot of tender beans, fluffy steamed rice, or a succulent roast? A pressure cooker does all these things efficiently and in about a third less time than conventional cooking methods.

Primary Uses

Pressure cookers excel at making hot, delicious dishes:

COOKING WITH LIQUIDS   Soups and stocks are ideal in pressure cookers, but cooking in liquids is more than just these dishes. Anything cooked in wine, milk, beer, or water falls into this category, too—think sauerbraten, pork cooked in milk, and coq au vin. Flavored liquids add more flavor to the dish and also tenderize meats.

STEAMING   In conjunction with a steamer basket or trivet, steaming foods in a pressure cooker is one of the tastiest ways to cook vegetables and retain many of their essential vitamins and minerals. But because the cooker cooks so quickly, not all vegetables should be cooked this way. Some more delicate vegetables quickly turn to mush in the pressure cooker.

BRAISING AND POT ROASTING   In traditional cooking, braising and cooking with liquids are in the same category. But because you can use less liquid in a pressure cooker, braising is a category on its own, and the sauce that's generally served with the dish becomes so intense inside the pressure cooker, you don't have to reduce it on the stovetop. Pot roasting can be done in a pressure cooker, too, using even less liquid than required for braising.

CANNING   Canning is another primary use for the pressure cooker. In fact, it's the only way the U.S. Department of Agriculture recommends canning low-acid foods at home. Not all pressure *cookers* are pressure *canners*, though. It has to have a 15 PSI setting, and it must be able to maintain such a setting for the entire cook time in order to can. Combo cooker/canners are available that can do both.

Foods to Pressure Cook

MEAT
Animal proteins of all kinds become tender and stay moist in a pressure cooker.

LEGUMES
Dried beans cook faster, retain their shape, and become perfectly tender with very little hassle.

WHOLE GRAINS
From whole grains to ground, from farro to oats, cooking grains under pressure is quicker and easier than via conventional methods.

Secondary Uses

Your pressure cooker also can tackle these tasks:

JUICE EXTRACTION Outfitting your pressure cooker with a trivet and adding some strawberries and a small amount of water is a quick and easy way to extract juice, especially from berries.

DISTILLING Anytime you create steam from a liquid, you can distill. You'd have to use a traditional rather than electric cooker and modify it a bit, but you can use your pressure cooker to distill flowers and other aromatics to make infused waters, such as orange water or rose water.

STERILIZING Your pressure cooker also can sterilize glass jars, glass baby bottles, and anything else that might need to be sanitized, as long as it fits into the cooker with the lid on and won't melt under heat.

> Electric stoves take time to cool, so when cooking with a traditional pressure cooker on an electric stove, use two burners—one set to the higher heat called for in the recipe, and the other set to low. Then slide your cooker from the high-heat burner to the low-heat one as necessary.

Foods Not to Pressure Cook

PASTA
Cooking pasta under pressure isn't really any quicker than traditional methods, and many times the results are less than spectacular.

TENDER VEGETABLES
Small, young, tender asparagus, baby green beans, baby spinach, fresh peas, and similar foods overcook in the pressure cooker.

FRIED FOOD
You can use your pressure cooker to fry foods as long as you have the lid off. Never fry foods under pressure.

Types of **Pressure Cookers**

Pressure cookers come in three primary types but with many variations among them. Maybe you've inherited an old cooker, or maybe you're shopping for a new cooker, either stovetop or electric. Let's look at what you need to know to make the right choice, or make the best use of the cooker you have.

Old Stovetop Cookers

Traditional first-generation stovetop pressure cookers did everything from canning winter stores to cooking perfectly tender roasts. Many were made of aluminum, with lids that screwed down tight, and were large enough to hold ½-gallon (2l) canning jars.

These cookers contained just one pressure valve, which was really more of a vent you placed different weights on top of to set the pressure, so they hissed steam and the valves jiggled as you cooked. Because they used a single valve, the old cookers weren't especially safe and were prone to failure. Mostly the lids popped off and food splattered everywhere. Many older models were preset at 15 PSI; new models sometimes allow you to set any pressure with a valve.

Still, if you keep the valve openings clear of debris and the gaskets supple, and when used properly and with requisite caution, these cookers are safe.

New Stovetop Cookers

Second-generation traditional cookers look similar to their predecessors, but they're quite different. With more safety features, modern stovetop pressure cookers are nearly foolproof.

Today's cookers work silently, are nonventing, and hiss only when the internal pressure becomes too high. The spring-loaded valves are used for safety only, as is the rubber seal housed in the lid. Many cookers have a heat-conducting bottom plate that disperses heat evenly. This allows you to bring the cooker to pressure and reduce the heat to low while still maintaining pressure. They often allow two pressure settings, 8 PSI (level 1 for traditional cookers and low for electric cookers) or 15 PSI (level 2 for traditional cookers and high for electric cookers).

Second-generation stovetop cookers are highly versatile and come in sizes to fit most home cooks' needs: 3.5 quart (3.5l), 4 quart (4l), 5 quart (5l), 6 quart (5.5l), and 8 quart (8l). Usually, you can use a larger-size cooker than the recipe calls for.

Electric Cookers

The newest type of pressure cooker, many electric pressure cookers serve as multifunctional cookers: slow cookers, steamers, rice cookers, and pressure cookers all in one appliance. They work in a similar way to the new stovetop varieties, with a nonstick insert that's sealed under pressure. You set the temperature (either low or high) and pressure on a control panel on the side of the cooker.

The appeal of electric cookers is their ease and convenience. You program the cooker for stew, and it sets the time and pressure for you. Many of these cookers also have automatic on/off, warming functions, as well as other control panel settings.

Some of these cookers have drawbacks, however. There's no cold water release capability, some don't offer a sauté mode, and the pressure settings vary from one brand to another. If you plan to do any low-acid canning, this is not the right cooker to purchase.

PRESSURE COOKER ACCESSORIES

When considering a pressure cooker to purchase, think about how you'll use it. This helps you choose the best size for your needs and also identify necessary accessories, such as perforated steamer baskets, trivets, canning equipment, and baking pans. Each one of these items has multiple uses, and you can probably discover many more as you gain pressure cooking experience.

STEAMER BASKET

TRIVET

CANNING RACK

Safety and **Maintenance**

Stories abound about pressure cookers "blowing up," and surely there were many cookers whose lids came off and the contents spattered all over. But with modern technology, precision manufacturing, and multiple safety valves, modern pressure cookers are as safe as any other kitchen appliance.

Safety Checklist

Keep the following safety points in mind when using your pressure cooker:

☐ Always remove the rubber gasket, check for cracks, and be sure it isn't overly brittle from use. Replace the gasket if needed.

☐ Check valves for any obstructions like grit or sticky residue left behind by food, and clean as necessary.

☐ If you hear a hiss, that means too much pressure has built up inside the cooker, usually because the heat wasn't reduced in time or to a low-enough temperature. Reduce the heat, and the hiss should stop as soon as the pressure drops.

☐ If you're having difficulty getting to pressure, check to be sure the lid is on properly, there's water in the pan, and the gasket is properly sealing.

☐ Do not leave your pressure cooker unattended.

Maintenance and Cleaning

Always clean your pressure cooker thoroughly after each use. Remove the gasket, clean it with a soft sponge and a mild detergent, and let it air-dry. Clean under the rim of the lid, and rinse well to remove any grit or food grime. Hand-wash the rest of the lid, and dry the lid completely.

Clean the pot by hand, too, using a sponge and a soft-bristled brush if needed. Take special care to ensure the bayonet mounts for the lid (the tabs that lock the lid in place) are free of debris. Dry the pot completely.

If there's tough debris or burnt-on grime in your pressure cooker, soak it before cleaning to loosen the dirt. To deal with really tough problems, fill the pot, bring the water to a boil, and clean the pot as directed.

Avoid using harsh detergents and scratch pads on your pressure cooker, and don't clean any parts of it in the dishwasher.

Cautions

With some care and common sense, you'll have years of successful pressure cooking. Here are some cautions to keep in mind:

- **DON'T OVERFILL WITH WATER.** Filling your pressure cooker more than two thirds full risks clogging the valves.

- **DON'T OVERPACK WITH FOOD.** An overly full pressure cooker won't cook the food inside evenly or efficiently. Never fill your pressure cooker more than two thirds full, and take into consideration the liquid content of your dish and the density of the ingredients.

- **BEWARE OF THE STEAM.** Steam is always present with pressure cooking, and it can burn your skin quickly. If you take a few precautions, however, you shouldn't have any problems.

  Most pressure cookers are designed to usher steam away from you. The quick-release valve moves the steam in the opposite direction of the handle, or anywhere your hand might reasonably be while handling a pot. However, never remove the lid while the pot is under pressure, and don't force the lid open. When you do open the lid, always use it as a shield for your hands and body by tilting up the far side of the lid as you open the pan, leaving the edge closest to you in contact with the edge of the pot. This pushes the steam away from you rather than allowing it to billow up in your face.

Release **Methods**

Releasing the pressure in your pressure cooker correctly and safely is essential for safety and to keep the food inside from overcooking. There are three basic methods to release pressure: cold water, quick, and natural. (Be sure to read the manual for your specific pressure cooker for more information.)

Cold Water Release

At about 15 seconds, this is the fastest way to cool your traditional pressure cooker to a temperature low enough to safely open the lid. (This method is not suitable for electric pressure cookers because they should not be doused with water.) It's most often used with quick-cooking foods so you can get them out of the pot before they overcook.

To release pressure using the cold water method, transfer your traditional pressure cooker to the sink and position it so water runs only over the edge of the lid. Turn on the cold water, and carefully rotate the cooker in the sink, avoiding running water over the valve.

Quick Release

One of the nice things about the quick release method, which takes about 1 or 2 minutes, is that there's no need to carry the cooker to the sink. If you're cooking tender vegetables such as broccoli and need to get them out of the pot immediately so they don't overcook, it's best to use the cold water release method because it's almost instant. But for most other foods, the quick release method is fine and enables you to get food to the table while it's still hot.

To release pressure using the quick release method, first remove the pressure cooker from heat or turn off the burner. Then, depending on the type of cooker you have, either turn the pressure knob so the cooker can release the steam at its own pace, or place a long-handled wooden spoon on the spring-loaded valve to release the steam. The spoon enables you to keep your hands a safe distance away from the escaping steam—and a possible burn.

Natural Release

The natural release method is by far the simplest, but it's also the least used in because it can take 25 to 30 minutes or longer for the pot to cool, and some foods can overcook in the process. (This method is widely used for canning, however.)

To release pressure using the natural release method, simply remove the pot from heat and let it cool on its own.

Never run water directly over the valve, or you could compromise its integrity and reliability. Never submerge any pressure cooker in water. Never run water over an electric cooker. And no matter which type of cooker you have, mind the steam and stay out of harm's way.

COLD WATER RELEASE METHOD

Using the handles, carry the pressure cooker to an empty sink. (Remember, this method does not apply to electric cookers.) Place the cooker so the pressure valve is not directly under the faucet, turn on the cold water, and run the water over the edges of the lid and down the sides of the pot, carefully rotating the cooker under the water. When the pressure gauge indicates the temperature has dropped low enough that the lid can be safely removed, remove the cooker from the sink, and remove the lid.

QUICK RELEASE METHOD

Remove the pressure cooker from heat, and use the quick release valve to release the pressure. If the valve starts to spit moisture, pause for 5 seconds and release the valve again. When the pressure is fully released, remove the lid, being mindful of the hot steam.

Understanding **PSI**

PSI stands for *pounds per square inch,* and it's a measure of the pressure within a pressure cooker. Higher pressure makes food cook faster and more evenly. Take a minute to learn about PSI, and in the future, all you'll need to think about is whether to set the pressure cooker to level 1 for traditional cookers/low for electric cookers or level 2 for traditional cookers/high for electric cookers.

What Is PSI?

The science of pressure cooking isn't complicated: when boiling water and steam are put under pressure, they become the same temperature. Apply additional heat, the pressure builds, and you get higher temperatures. What this means for you and your pressure cooker is that your food cooks evenly and from all sides. That's what makes pressure cooking different from almost all other methods of cooking. It's also what makes it very efficient.

Water boils at 212°F (100°C). Steam, because it's water in gas form, is even hotter. But under pressure, water becomes superheated. At 8 PSI, water reaches 235°F (115°C) before it boils, and the resulting steam is the same temperature. At 15 PSI, water boils at 250°F (120°C).

Temperature and Pressure

Left uncontrolled and under pressure, the water and steam will continue to rise in temperature. But a valve set to a specified release pressure allows steam to escape, maintaining a given PSI and, therefore, a given temperature, inside the pressure cooker.

Think of PSI as your temperature knob on the stove: low, medium, and high. Different pressures control the heat inside the pot.

The Importance of Time

Time plays a key role in pressure cooking, and it's crucial that you adhere to the times specified in the recipes. A pressure cooker left to its own devices can obliterate foods into a mushy mess very quickly.

Pressure cooking times begin when the PSI in the recipe is reached. That's why it's important to bring liquids to a boil first, lock on the lid, and wait until the pressure gauge reaches the desired PSI. Only then should you start the timer.

Adjusting for Altitude

If, due to where you live, you often make altitude adjustments to recipes when cooking, you'll need to make some modifications when pressure cooking, too.

If you live above 2,000 feet (610m) elevation above sea level, you'll need to change your pressure cooker cook times. The rule is a 5 percent increase in cooking time for every 1,000-foot (305m) increase in altitude over 2,000 feet (610m). So at 3,000 feet (915m), an increase of 5 percent is needed. At 4,000 feet (1,220m), it jumps to 10 percent, and so on, as shown in the accompanying table.

Altitude also affects how much cooking liquid you need. If the altitude requires a 5 percent cook time increase, the liquid requirements increase by 2.5 percent, or half the altitude increase. So if a recipe calls for ½ cup water, you'll need ¾ cup. There are no hard-and-fast rules on how much more liquid you need when adjusting for altitude because it somewhat depends on how much liquid will be released by the ingredients being cooked. The table here offers good starting points.

ALTITUDE ADJUSTMENTS

ALTITUDE	INCREASE IN COOK TIME	INCREASE IN LIQUID
3,000 feet (915m)	5%	2.5%
4,000 feet (1,220m)	10%	5%
5,000 feet (1,525m)	15%	7.5%
6,000 feet (1,830m)	20%	10%
7,000 feet (2,135m)	25%	12.5%
8,000 feet (2,440m)	30%	n/a
9,000 feet (2,745m)	35%	n/a
10,000 feet (3,050m)	40%	n/a

Pressure Cooking **Vegetables**

A steaming bowl of vegetables cooked perfectly in a pressure cooker always arrives at the table looking vibrant and nutritious. A pressure cooker is a superstar when it comes to cooking vegetables fast while retaining vitamins and flavor.

Size Matters

Try to cut vegetables the same size so they finish cooking at the same time. Also keep in mind what else you might be cooking with the vegetables, like stew meat for example, and overall cooking times. You might want to cut the vegetables larger or even leave them whole so they finish cooking at the same time as the stew meat. And remember, you can always cook in stages so the vegetables aren't overcooked and the meats still become tender.

QUICK-COOKING VEGGIES

Some more delicate vegetables require less cook time. When a recipe calls for broccoli, asparagus, or spinach, for example, you can stop the cooking process near the end of the time specified, release the pressure, remove the lid, add the quick-cooking vegetables, and continue with the recipe.

CARROTS CUT INTO 1-INCH (2.5CM) CYLINDERS ARE BEST FOR QUICK-COOKING STEWS. TRY TO CUT ANY MEAT IN THE DISH INTO PIECES THAT WILL COOK IN THE SAME AMOUNT OF TIME.

FINGERLING POTATOES ARE GREAT FOR PRESSURE COOKING. JUST CUT IN HALF LENGTHWISE—NO PEELING NECESSARY.

PRESSURE COOKING POTATOES

Potatoes fare well when pressure cooked. The cook time depends on many variables: will the potatoes be cut, halved, cooked whole, peeled or not, mashed, used in potato salad, etc. Be sure to follow your recipe carefully when pressure cooking potatoes.

TRIVETS AND STEAMER BASKETS

When steaming vegetables, use a trivet or steamer basket, and always add as little water as your cooker allows to still operate safely. This is often ½ to ¾ cup.

DO NOT OVERFILL

To ensure even cooking, do not overfill the steamer basket with vegetables. The key is to leave enough space around the food so the steam can get into all the nooks and crannies. Flat cuts such as potato rounds are especially prone to undercooking because they can stick together.

Trivet

Steamer Basket

It might take a bit of practice until you can produce properly cooked vegetables. Be patient, and pay attention to the cooking process. Make mental notes as you work, and above all else, keep trying.

Pressure Cooking
Meat

Save the expensive, tender cuts of meat for the grill. Your pressure cooker transforms lesser, inexpensive cuts of meat into great-tasting stews, succulent braises, and tender pot roasts.

But just because a pressure cooker does wonders with inexpensive cuts of meat doesn't mean you can use *cheap* meat. If a cut has a lot of sinew (or silverskin), remove it with a knife before cooking. Also remove any bruised or discolored areas you see. Let pressure cooked meat rest for 10 minutes before slicing or shredding it to allow the collagen in the meat to relax, making the meat more tender. And always slice meat against the grain.

Choosing and Prepping Meat

Perhaps the most important thing to look for when buying red meat for the pressure cooker is marbling, or fat content. Choose pieces that contain lots of white veins throughout. Fat is what flavors meat, and even in a pressure cooker, meat without the right fat content can become dry.

It's also a good idea to season meat with salt up to 24 hours before pressure cooking it. This gives the salt time to penetrate the meat's protein, which enhances the flavor and helps the meat retain moisture.

Meat browns better if the surface is dry. At the very least, pat meat dry with a paper towel before searing.

CHICKEN
It's almost easier to cook a whole bird and pull the meat off the bone than pressure cook boneless breasts.

STEW MEAT
This can be of any cut of meat. It cooks best when cut into 1×1-inch (2.5×2.5cm) cubes.

SHANKS
Lamb, beef, and veal shanks become tender and flavorful in no time.

CHICKEN Whole chickens do very well in the pressure cooker. A 3-pound (1.5kg) chicken cooks to tender quickly and easily. Bone-in thighs and legs are fantastic as well.

BEEF Chuck roasts are great for the pressure cooker. Left whole, cut into stew meat, or ground for meatballs, the fat-to-protein ratio is ideal, and they become tender and juicy in no time.

PORK Pork, cured and fresh, is perfect for the pressure cooker. Be aware that bacon cooked under pressure for long periods of time develops an odd texture. To overcome this, remove the bacon after rendering it crispy and put it back at the end of the cook time to warm.

SEAFOOD Seafood cooks very fast under pressure, which makes it ideal for busy weeknight meals. Opt for firmer fish like tuna, salmon, and mackerel that can be cut into 1-inch (2.5cm) cubes for curries and Asian-style dishes. Your pressure cooker also makes short work of shellfish.

Pressure Cooker Frying

You can use your pressure cooker for sautéing, to sear meats before adding the liquids and other ingredients and locking on the lid. However, you should never put large amounts of hot oil under pressure by locking on the lid, as you would for fried chicken. This is dangerous because the heat builds up quickly, the valves become clogged with oil, and the rubber seals can become compromised, all of which can cause failure and the possibility of an explosion.

PORK
Thin strips of pork, beef, and chicken pressure cook quickly in about 10 minutes.

ROASTS
Roasts of all kinds are great in the pressure cooker.

SEAFOOD
Fish and other seafood require a very short cook time in the pressure cooker.

Converting Conventional Recipes

Adapting your favorite recipes for pressure cooking isn't complicated. In fact, as you realize how much time pressure cooking saves you over conventional methods, and as you become comfortable and familiar with operating a pressure cooker, you'll be able to make these conversions pretty easily.

Conversion Tips

Use these tips to help you adapt traditional recipes to the pressure cooker:

ADD DAIRY LATER   With the exception of baked dishes such as cakes and custards, it's often best to add dairy at the end of the cook time to keep it from curdling or scorching.

COOK IN PHASES   Cook the meat first, release the pressure and open the cooker, add the vegetables, replace the lid, and finish cooking.

TIER INGREDIENTS   Stack multiple steamer baskets inside your pressure cooker to cook your main dish and sides simultaneously and keep the flavors separate.

USE PANS   Pour cake batter into a baking pan, cover it with aluminum foil, and bake it in your pressure cooker.

ADJUST THE WATER   Foods give off a lot of liquid under pressure, and it can't evaporate inside the sealed cooker. So when converting, use far less liquid than in the original recipe—often 1 cup total is sufficient.

REDUCE FOAMING   Some foods like rice, beans, and other starches foam when cooked. Add 1 teaspoon oil or fat to reduce the amount of foam and avoid clogging the valve.

BURN OFF ALCOHOL   If you're cooking with wine, burn off the alcohol before locking on the lid. Otherwise, the vapors stay trapped inside the cooker, and the wine remains raw.

AVOID OVERFILLING   Never fill a pressure cooker more than two thirds full. Overfilling yields an unevenly and incompletely cooked final dish.

REDUCE THE COOK TIME   Under pressure at 15 PSI, food often cooks in a third of the time of traditional methods. If it takes an hour conventionally, it'll take 20 minutes under pressure. Still, look for a recipe that's similar to the one you're converting to check the recommended time.

USE YOUR MANUAL   Make use of your owner's manual cook time and other charts. By looking at the different PSI and cook times of individual ingredients, you can figure out the best way to cook a traditional recipe in your pressure cooker.

Preparation Tips

Here are some helpful hints to keep in mind while preparing a dish:

VEGETABLES Grated and small-cut vegetables don't fare well under pressure. The appropriate-size cut is key to pressure cooking success. When preparing vegetables, look at the cook time and cut sizes and try to match them so everything cooks evenly and in the same amount of time. Or cook food in stages if need be.

MEATS Bone-in meats are more flavorful, and it's a good idea to use them whenever you can. When that's not possible and the meat needs to be cubed (not all does), a 1-inch (2.5cm) square piece is the minimum size.

Also, brown meat first before adding any other ingredients. You can remove it from the cooker after browning and before sautéing any vegetables and return it later when you're ready to lock on the lid.

CHICKEN Chicken is hard to cut off the bone, but often it's best to cook the chicken first, remove it from the pot, pick off the meat, and return the meat to the pot. Chicken can be cooked with skin on or off for almost all recipes. Skin adds lots of flavor, but not everyone likes it.

Stocking Your **Kitchen**

Stocking your kitchen for pressure cooking makes preparing weekday meals quicker and easier. In addition to the meats mentioned earlier, whole grains, beans, and other long-cooking ingredients often reserved for weekends, when time constraints are fewer, can now become midweek meals.

Grains

Whole grains, ancient grains, and gluten-free grains are widely available. Oat groats, farro, wheat berries, spelt, buckwheat, millet, and quinoa (which is actually a seed but is cooked like a grain) are all well suited to pressure cooking. Brown rice, farro, and spelt are best stored in the freezer, but others are just fine on the pantry shelf.

Whole grains contain more nutrients than processed versions, have a lower glycemic index, and are absorbed at a slower rate in your body. With your pressure cooker, you can easily add these good-for-you ingredients to more meals.

Beans

Cooking dried beans in your pressure cooker is faster, easier, and less expensive; requires less hands-on work than traditional cooking; and yields a better-tasting result. Try a variety of heirloom and standard varieties such as black turtle beans, pinto beans, cannellini beans, lentils (especially du Puy), and chickpeas.

Don't fret if you forget to soak beans overnight. You can quick soak dried beans by covering them in 4 cups water for every 1 cup dried beans and pressure cook for 2 minutes at level 2 for traditional cookers or on high for electric cookers. Use the cold water release method for traditional cookers and the quick release method for electric cookers, drain the beans, and continue as directed in your recipe.

Spices and Herbs

Pressure cooking produces flavorful foods, but you'll still want to season with spices and herbs.

Stock up on bay leaves, chili powder, cloves, cocoa powder, cumin, curry powder, ginger, kosher salt, paprika, vanilla extract (vanilla paste is really wonderful), and whole black peppercorns (a grinder, too) as well as fresh and dried herbs like oregano, rosemary, and thyme. Spice blends like Old Bay or a Cajun blend are also nice to have.

Salt is by far the most powerful flavoring tool in the kitchen and can do so many things, from flavoring to curing. Many types are available, and to decide which is best, you can do a tasting. Table salt with iodine is often very bitter, kosher salt has a mild taste and is clear when it dissolves, and sea salt comes in many flavors and prices. The recipes in this book use kosher salt. If you use iodized table salt instead, use half as much as what's called for. And before adding more salt to a dish, do a quick taste test. If a recipe calls for a pinch of salt, use your thumb and index finger to measure. For a two-finger pinch, use your thumb, index finger, and middle finger.

Produce

Storage vegetables stay fresh for weeks in the refrigerator or root cellar and can be pressure cooked for fast, hearty dishes. Carrots, celery, garlic, onions, and potatoes are excellent to have on hand. Also consider bell peppers, chiles, and green onions.

For fruit, stock dried apples, apricots, blueberries, cherries, cranberries, prunes, raisins, and about anything else you like. These cook quick in compotes, can be made into spreads, and are a great addition to puddings.

Planning **Weeknight Meals**

Creating a menu plan makes cooking nutritious meals throughout the week easy, helps you maximize your time, and uses up leftovers. Your pressure cooker can make quick and easy work of cooking your week's meals.

Chicken

Chicken is so versatile, and cooking whole chickens in your pressure cooker is very quick: a 3-pound (1.5kg) bird cooks in as little as 15 to 20 minutes. If your pressure cooker is big enough (8 quarts; 7.5l or larger), you can cook two birds at once.

CHICKEN AND DUMPLINGS   *Chicken and Dumplings* is a comfort food classic, and cooking two chickens yields an intense broth, with plenty of extra broth you can use throughout the week. If you don't use it all right away, freeze it for later.

CHICKEN SALAD   After you've pulled the chicken from the bones, you have a stockpile of meat you can use in many dishes. Try *Chicken Salad Deluxe*. It's good as a lunch or light dinner.

CHICKEN TACOS   Leftover chicken is perfect for chicken tacos. Try it in *Pressure Cooker Tacos*. Refer to the recipe for toppings, or create your own.

Beef

Cuts of beef that shred well (think chuck, flank, and brisket) make versatile weeknight meal options.

BRISKET   *Classic Beef Brisket* is a dinnertime staple. Tender and coated with *au jus* and melted onions, brisket is perfect in the pressure cooker. Double the amount to get more meals out of this cut.

SOUP   Make *Mushroom Barley Soup* more of a meal by adding shredded beef. Serve with a salad and some good bread.

BARBECUE   Warm up leftover shredded beef in leftover *au jus* and add your favorite barbecue sauce. Toast some buns, make some fresh and tangy coleslaw, and you have a great weeknight meal.

Pork

You have many options when it comes to pork. Use a butt roast, or two, and you have the basis of many fast and flavorful weeknight dishes.

PULLED PORK   Cook a double batch of *Southern-Style Pulled Pork*, add sauce to only what you're going to eat that night, and save the rest for other meals.

PORK RAMEN   Having pulled pork on hand makes it easy to prepare quick and easy pressure cooked *Pork Ramen*.

THAI-STYLE GREEN CURRY PORK   Of course, you could do something completely different and make the *Thai-Style Green Curry Chicken* and substitute pork for the chicken. Simply make the broth and add the pork at the end to warm it through.

Grains and Vegetables

Pressure cooked grains and vegetables are so much more colorful and vibrant, and they retain much of their flavor and vitamins. Beans, too. It's so easy to pressure cook a big batch once and use them in various healthy, filling salads or side dishes all week long.

RICE PILAF   Cook a double pot of *Basmati Rice Pilaf*, and use it as a side dish for several weeknight dinners.

VEGETABLE BURRITOS OR MEXICAN BOWLS   Having rice on hand enables you to make burritos, either vegetarian or with meat. Simply warm tortillas, spread on some warm rice, and top with your favorite burrito ingredients. Or make a Mexican bowl and skip the tortilla altogether.

CABBAGE, RICE, AND LENTILS   Make *One-Pot Cabbage, Rice, and Lentils* by adding the rice at the end, warming it through, and not allowing it to overcook. You also can add some shredded brisket with the rice for the meat lovers in your family.

pressure cooker
recipes

basics

From fresh stocks to easy dried beans, the basic, staple recipes in this section get you started with your pressure cooker and help you build your pressure cooking expertise.

Homemade beef stock is **rich** and **flavorful.** Use it as a base for **soups,** reduce it for rich **sauces,** or drink a **hot cup to warm you** on chilly days.

Rich Beef Stock

| 16 (1 CUP) SERVINGS | 15 MINUTES | 55 MINUTES | 2/HIGH |

INGREDIENTS

- 4 lb. (2kg) meaty beef bones
- 1 large white onion, cut into quarters (1½ cups)
- 2 large carrots, peeled and cut into 1-in. (2.5cm) chunks (¾ cup)
- 4 medium stalks celery, chopped (¾ cup)
- 2 tsp. whole black peppercorns
- 1 bay leaf
- 2 TB. fresh flat-leaf parsley
- 16 cups cold water

METHOD

1 In an 8-quart (7.5l) pressure cooker, combine meaty beef bones, white onion, carrots, celery, black peppercorns, bay leaf, and flat-leaf parsley. Carefully pour in cold water, set heat to medium (traditional)/high (electric), and bring to a boil.

2 Lock on the lid, and bring pressure to level 2 (traditional)/high (electric). Reduce heat to low, and cook at 2/high for 55 minutes. Turn off heat, let cool, perform a natural release, and remove the lid.

3 Strain stock with a fine mesh strainer. Use within 3 to 5 days, can in jars, or freeze.

NUTRITION PER SERVING

| Calories: 72 | Sugars: 4g | Protein: 5g | Cholesterol: 18mg |
| Carbohydrates: 5g | Dietary fiber: 2g | Fat: 2g | Sodium: 90mg |

Homemade chicken stock is **rich, flavorful,** and **filling.** Leave on the onion skin when making this version; it helps produce a nice, **golden-colored stock.**

Chicken Stock

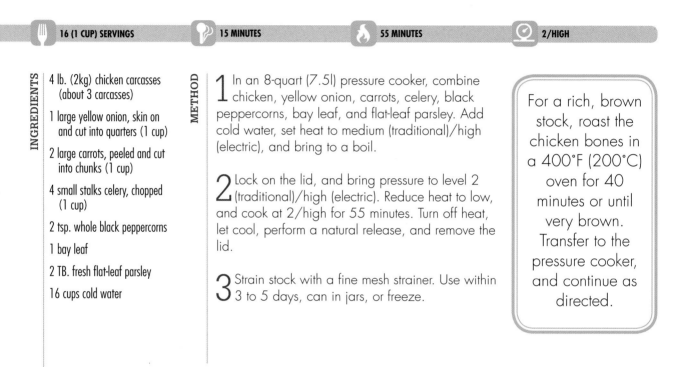

| 16 (1 CUP) SERVINGS | 15 MINUTES | 55 MINUTES | 2/HIGH |

INGREDIENTS

4 lb. (2kg) chicken carcasses (about 3 carcasses)

1 large yellow onion, skin on and cut into quarters (1 cup)

2 large carrots, peeled and cut into chunks (1 cup)

4 small stalks celery, chopped (1 cup)

2 tsp. whole black peppercorns

1 bay leaf

2 TB. fresh flat-leaf parsley

16 cups cold water

METHOD

1 In an 8-quart (7.5l) pressure cooker, combine chicken, yellow onion, carrots, celery, black peppercorns, bay leaf, and flat-leaf parsley. Add cold water, set heat to medium (traditional)/high (electric), and bring to a boil.

2 Lock on the lid, and bring pressure to level 2 (traditional)/high (electric). Reduce heat to low, and cook at 2/high for 55 minutes. Turn off heat, let cool, perform a natural release, and remove the lid.

3 Strain stock with a fine mesh strainer. Use within 3 to 5 days, can in jars, or freeze.

For a rich, brown stock, roast the chicken bones in a 400°F (200°C) oven for 40 minutes or until very brown. Transfer to the pressure cooker, and continue as directed.

NUTRITION PER SERVING

Calories: **12**	Sugars: **0g**	Protein: **1g**	Cholesterol: **0mg**
Carbohydrates: **2g**	Dietary fiber: **0g**	Fat: **.3g**	Sodium: **130mg**

Making a **vegetable stock** that doesn't turn out sweet and oniony can be tricky. For best results, use **tomatoes** and dried mushrooms such as **shiitakes.**

Vegetable Stock

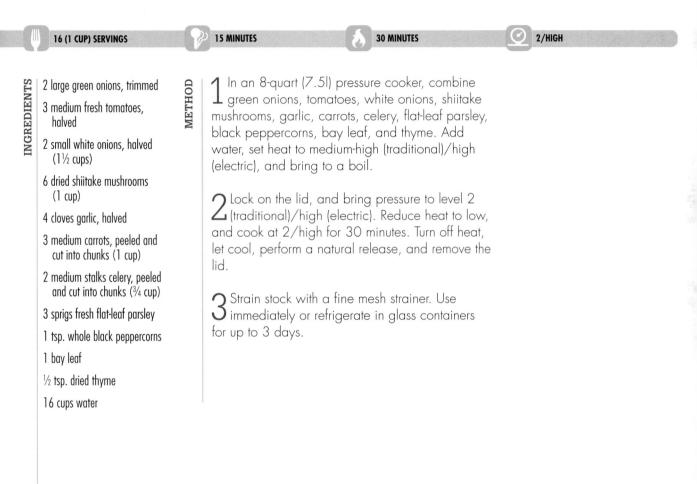

🍴 16 (1 CUP) SERVINGS	🥄 15 MINUTES	🔥 30 MINUTES	⏲ 2/HIGH

INGREDIENTS

2 large green onions, trimmed

3 medium fresh tomatoes, halved

2 small white onions, halved (1½ cups)

6 dried shiitake mushrooms (1 cup)

4 cloves garlic, halved

3 medium carrots, peeled and cut into chunks (1 cup)

2 medium stalks celery, peeled and cut into chunks (¾ cup)

3 sprigs fresh flat-leaf parsley

1 tsp. whole black peppercorns

1 bay leaf

½ tsp. dried thyme

16 cups water

METHOD

1 In an 8-quart (7.5l) pressure cooker, combine green onions, tomatoes, white onions, shiitake mushrooms, garlic, carrots, celery, flat-leaf parsley, black peppercorns, bay leaf, and thyme. Add water, set heat to medium-high (traditional)/high (electric), and bring to a boil.

2 Lock on the lid, and bring pressure to level 2 (traditional)/high (electric). Reduce heat to low, and cook at 2/high for 30 minutes. Turn off heat, let cool, perform a natural release, and remove the lid.

3 Strain stock with a fine mesh strainer. Use immediately or refrigerate in glass containers for up to 3 days.

NUTRITION PER SERVING

Calories: **15**	Sugars: **2g**	Protein: **0g**	Cholesterol: **0mg**
Carbohydrates: **3g**	Dietary fiber: **1g**	Fat: **0g**	Sodium: **140mg**

Pressure cooked eggs **peel perfectly,** the cooking times are **more exact,** and you don't get a sulfur ring around the **yolk.**

Pressure Cooker **Eggs**

🍴 1 EGG PER SERVING	🕐 5 MINUTES	🔥 VARIES	⏲ 2/HIGH

INGREDIENTS

Large eggs, cool (34°F; 1°C)

METHOD

1 Add a trivet or steamer basket to any size pressure cooker, and add the minimum amount of water allowed for your cooker. Set heat to medium-high (traditional)/high (electric), add eggs to trivet or basket, and bring to a boil.

2 Lock on the lid, bring pressure to level 2 (traditional)/high (electric), and cook as directed for egg doneness (see accompanying table). Remove from (traditional)/turn off (electric) heat, perform a cold water (traditional)/quick (electric) release, and remove the lid.

3 Serve soft- and medium-boiled eggs immediately.

4 For hard-boiled, remove eggs from the cooker and immediately plunge in an ice-water bath. Cool eggs completely, drain, dry, and peel as needed.

EGG DONENESS	COOK TIME
Soft yolk	3 minutes
Medium yolk	4 minutes
Hard boiled	6 minutes

I keep six bottle caps in my kitchen to use for egg stands when pressure cooking. Standing the eggs fat end down on the upturned bottle caps gives them the perfect finished shape, which is great for making deviled eggs.

NUTRITION PER SERVING

Calories: **72**
Carbohydrates: **.5g**
Sugars: **0g**
Dietary fiber: **0g**
Protein: **6g**
Fat: **5g**
Cholesterol: **186mg**
Sodium: **71mg**

Your pressure cooker cooks rice to **tender** and **fluffy perfection.** For best results, find a **brand** and **type** of rice you like and stick with it.

Pressure Cooker **Rice**

🍴 8 (1 CUP) SERVINGS	⏱ 5 MINUTES	🔥 5 MINUTES	⏲ 2/HIGH

INGREDIENTS

2 cups jasmine rice

3 cups water

1½ tsp. vegetable oil or unsalted butter

METHOD

1 In a 4-quart (4l) pressure cooker, combine jasmine rice, water, and vegetable oil. Set heat to medium-high (traditional)/high (electric), and bring to a boil.

2 Lock on the lid, bring pressure to level 2 (traditional)/high (electric), and cook for 5 minutes. Remove from (traditional)/turn off (electric) heat, perform a cold water (traditional)/quick (electric) release, and remove the lid.

3 Serve hot. Refrigerate leftovers for up to 3 days, or freeze.

> For brown rice, use 2 cups brown jasmine rice, and cook it for 20 to 22 minutes at level 2/high.

NUTRITION PER SERVING

Calories: 170	Sugars: 0g	Protein: 3g	Cholesterol: 0mg
Carbohydrates: 36g	Dietary fiber: 1g	Fat: 1g	Sodium: 0mg

Cooking a simple pot of dried beans isn't difficult. **Soak** the beans overnight for a **faster** cook, and add salt before cooking for a more **flavorful** finished dish.

Easy **Dried Beans**

4 (½ CUP) SERVINGS	5 MINUTES + SOAK TIME	12 MINUTES	2/HIGH

INGREDIENTS

8 oz. (225g) dried pinto beans, washed, picked over, soaked overnight, and drained

1 small yellow onion, halved (½ cup)

1 tsp. kosher salt

1 TB. olive oil, lard, bacon grease, or unsalted butter

¼ tsp. freshly ground black pepper

Water

METHOD

1 In a 4-quart (4l) pressure cooker, combine pinto beans, yellow onion, kosher salt, olive oil, and black pepper. Add enough water to cover beans by 1 inch (2.5cm). Set heat to medium-high (traditional)/high (electric), and bring to a boil.

2 Lock on the lid, bring pressure to level 2 (traditional)/high (electric), and cook for 12 minutes. Remove from (traditional)/turn off (electric) heat, perform a natural release, and remove the lid.

3 Serve hot.

Instead of soaking overnight, a quick soak speeds up the process: combine 1 cup dried beans and 4 cups water in the pressure cooker, and set heat to medium-high (traditional)/high (electric). Lock on the lid, bring to pressure level 2 (traditional)/high (electric), and cook for 2 minutes. Remove from (traditional)/turn off (electric) heat, perform a natural release, and proceed as directed.

NUTRITION PER SERVING

Calories: 230	Sugars: 2g	Protein: 14g	Cholesterol: 0mg
Carbohydrates: 34g	Dietary fiber: 9g	Fat: 3.5g	Sodium: 490mg

This **all-purpose** tomato sauce is ideal for pasta. The vegetables provide plenty of **flavor** and **substance,** but feel free to add shredded beef or pork if you like.

Pressure Cooker **Pasta Sauce**

8 (½ CUP) SERVINGS	15 MINUTES	14 MINUTES	2/HIGH

INGREDIENTS

¼ cup extra-virgin olive oil

2 medium leeks, white and a little green parts, diced small (1¼ cups)

3 medium stalks celery, halved lengthwise and diced small (¾ cup)

2 medium carrots, peeled and diced small (¾ cup)

2 TB. minced garlic

½ tsp. kosher salt

¼ tsp. freshly ground white pepper

3 cups tomato sauce

1 (6-oz.; 175ml) can tomato paste

1 tsp. dried oregano

1 tsp. dried basil

½ tsp. dried thyme

Water

METHOD

1 In a 6-quart (5.5l) pressure cooker set to medium-high (traditional)/ high (electric) heat, heat extra-virgin olive oil. When hot, add leeks, celery, carrots, and garlic. Stir, season with kosher salt and white pepper, and cook for 4 minutes or until vegetables become soft but garlic doesn't brown.

2 Stir in tomato sauce, tomato paste, oregano, basil, and thyme, and bring sauce to a boil.

3 Lock on the lid, and bring pressure to level 2 (traditional)/high (electric). Reduce heat to low, and cook at 2/high for 14 minutes. Remove from (traditional)/turn off (electric) heat, perform a cold water (traditional)/quick (electric) release, and remove the lid.

4 Taste, and add more salt as necessary. If sauce is thicker than you like, add water 1 tablespoon at a time, stirring between each addition.

5 Serve hot. Refrigerate any leftovers in a jar for up to 1 week.

NUTRITION PER SERVING

Calories: 120	Sugars: 8g	Protein: 3g	Cholesterol: 0mg
Carbohydrates: 13g	Dietary fiber: 3g	Fat: 7g	Sodium: 790mg

breakfasts

Your pressure cooker makes cooking soft-boiled eggs, hard-boiled eggs, and custards quick and easy for breakfast. (Frying eggs in your pressure cooker isn't recommended.) It also makes short work of creamy, whole-grain cereals to get your morning started right.

Heavy cream makes these eggs **very rich**. Best reserved for special occasions rather than every day, they're ideal for **holiday brunches**.

Eggs en Cocotte à la Crème

🍴 4 (1 EGG) SERVINGS	⏲ 30 MINUTES	🔥 2 MINUTES	⏱ 2/HIGH

INGREDIENTS

8 tsp. heavy cream

4 large eggs, cool

½ tsp. kosher salt

8 medium asparagus spears, trimmed and root end peeled

4 slices prosciutto, halved lengthwise for 8 pieces

1 tsp. unsalted butter

1 medium green onion, minced (optional)

METHOD

1 Add a steamer basket to a 4-quart (4l) pressure cooker, and fill with the minimum amount of water allowed for your cooker.

2 Using ¼ teaspoon unsalted butter each, lightly grease 4 (4-ounce; 120ml) ramekins, espresso cups, or other heat-proof vessels. Pour 1 teaspoon heavy cream in each dish.

3 One at a time, crack 1 egg into each dish, season it with 1 pinch kosher salt, and pour another 1 teaspoon heavy cream on top of each egg. Cover each cup tightly with aluminum foil, and place cups in the steamer basket. Set heat to medium-high (traditional)/high (electric), and bring to a boil.

4 Lock on the lid, bring pressure to level 2 (traditional)/high (electric), and cook for 2 minutes. Remove from (traditional)/turn off (electric) heat, perform a cold water (traditional)/quick (electric) release, remove the lid, and carefully remove egg cups.

5 Meanwhile, spiral wrap each asparagus spear with 1 piece of prosciutto, and rub with ⅛ teaspoon unsalted butter each.

6 In a sauté pan over medium-high heat, sear prosciutto-asparagus spears for 3 minutes.

7 Place 1 egg cup on a plate with 2 spears asparagus to dip in yolks, garnish with green onion (if using), and serve.

NUTRITION PER SERVING

Calories: 150	Sugars: 1g	Protein: 10g	Cholesterol: 235mg
Carbohydrates: 3g	Dietary fiber: 1g	Fat: 12g	Sodium: 560mg

With their **shrimp** and **andouille sausage,** these egg cups are reminiscent of **New Orleans** and a **good jazz brunch.**

Egg **Cups**

6 (½ CUP) SERVINGS	30 MINUTES	17 MINUTES	2/HIGH

INGREDIENTS

1 TB. vegetable oil

6 shrimp (size 26 to 30), shelled, deveined, and diced small

½ small green bell pepper, ribs and seeds removed, and diced small (¼ cup)

1 small stalk celery, diced small (¼ cup)

1 small shallot, minced (¼ cup)

2 tsp. minced garlic

3 oz. (75g) cooked andouille sausage, diced small

½ cup whole milk

6 large eggs

½ tsp. kosher salt

¼ tsp. freshly ground black pepper

1 TB. fresh chives, chopped

METHOD

1 In a medium sauté pan over medium-high heat, heat vegetable oil. When hot, add shrimp, green bell pepper, celery, shallot, garlic, and andouille sausage, and sauté for about 4 minutes or until softened. Remove from heat.

2 In a large bowl, combine whole milk, eggs, kosher salt, and black pepper until eggs are smooth and blended.

3 Grease the bottoms and sides of 6 (4-ounce; 110g) ramekins with about 1 tablespoon unsalted butter. Divide shrimp and andouille filling among ramekins, cover each tightly with aluminum foil, and place in a steamer basket.

4 Add the basket to a 6-quart (5.5l) pressure cooker, and fill with the minimum amount of water allowed for your cooker. Do not allow water to touch bottom of ramekins. Set heat to high (traditional)/high (electric), and bring to a boil.

5 Lock on the lid, bring pressure to level 2 (traditional)/high (electric), and cook for 12 minutes. Remove from (traditional)/turn off (electric) heat, and set aside for 5 minutes. Perform a quick release, remove the lid, and lift out the steamer basket.

6 Uncover ramekins, top with chives, and serve.

NUTRITION PER SERVING

Calories: **140**	Sugars: **2g**	Protein: **8g**	Cholesterol: **235mg**
Carbohydrates: **5g**	Dietary fiber: **0g**	Fat: **10g**	Sodium: **250mg**

This **sweet** and **hearty** oatmeal is more like a **dessert** than breakfast. Pressure cooking steel-cut oats takes a **fraction of the time** conventional methods require.

Apple Cinnamon **Breakfast Oats**

	4 (½ CUP) SERVINGS		5 MINUTES		10 MINUTES		2/HIGH

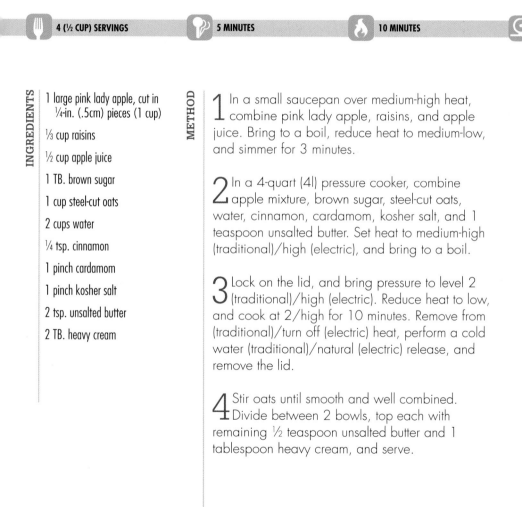

INGREDIENTS

1 large pink lady apple, cut in ¼-in. (.5cm) pieces (1 cup)

⅓ cup raisins

½ cup apple juice

1 TB. brown sugar

1 cup steel-cut oats

2 cups water

¼ tsp. cinnamon

1 pinch cardamom

1 pinch kosher salt

2 tsp. unsalted butter

2 TB. heavy cream

METHOD

1 In a small saucepan over medium-high heat, combine pink lady apple, raisins, and apple juice. Bring to a boil, reduce heat to medium-low, and simmer for 3 minutes.

2 In a 4-quart (4l) pressure cooker, combine apple mixture, brown sugar, steel-cut oats, water, cinnamon, cardamom, kosher salt, and 1 teaspoon unsalted butter. Set heat to medium-high (traditional)/high (electric), and bring to a boil.

3 Lock on the lid, and bring pressure to level 2 (traditional)/high (electric). Reduce heat to low, and cook at 2/high for 10 minutes. Remove from (traditional)/turn off (electric) heat, perform a cold water (traditional)/natural (electric) release, and remove the lid.

4 Stir oats until smooth and well combined. Divide between 2 bowls, top each with remaining ½ teaspoon unsalted butter and 1 tablespoon heavy cream, and serve.

NUTRITION PER SERVING

Calories: 280	Sugars: 22g	Protein: 7g	Cholesterol: 15mg
Carbohydrates: 52g	Dietary fiber: 6g	Fat: 7g	Sodium: 45mg

If sweet breakfasts aren't your thing, this **savory oatmeal** is a nice alternative. **Black pepper** and **Parmesan cheese** are a natural pairing with oats.

Savory Parmesan
Steel-Cut Oats

2 (1 CUP) SERVINGS	5 MINUTES	15 MINUTES	2/HIGH

INGREDIENTS

1 cup steel-cut oats

2 cups water

¼ tsp. kosher salt

1 TB. unsalted butter

4 TB. cup grated Parmesan cheese

1 TB. chopped fresh chives

¼ tsp. freshly ground black pepper

METHOD

1 Place steel-cut oats in a strainer, and rinse with cold running water.

2 Transfer oats to a 4-quart (4l) pressure cooker, and add water, kosher salt, and 1 teaspoon unsalted butter. Set heat to medium-high (traditional)/high (electric), and bring to a boil.

3 Lock on the lid, and bring pressure to level 2 (traditional)/high (electric). Reduce heat to low, and cook at 2/high for 15 minutes. Remove from (traditional)/turn off (electric) heat, perform a cold water (traditional)/quick (electric) release, and remove the lid.

4 Divide oats between 2 bowls. Evenly divide remaining unsalted butter, Parmesan cheese, chives, and black pepper over top, and serve.

> For protein-powered oats, pour 1 tablespoon hot beef broth over the top, cover with 1 fried egg, and serve.

NUTRITION PER SERVING

Calories: 370	Sugars: 0g	Protein: 16g	Cholesterol: 25mg
Carbohydrates: 54g	Dietary fiber: 8g	Fat: 14g	Sodium: 400mg

This hot, multigrain cereal is a **warm** and **comforting** start on cold mornings. It also makes a great **side dish** alongside braised meats.

Five-Grain **Oatmeal**

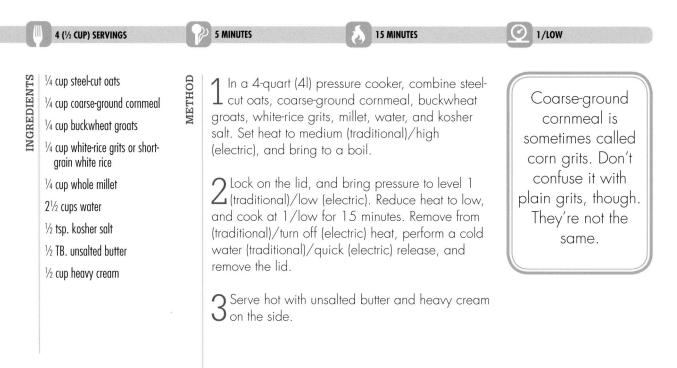

4 (½ CUP) SERVINGS | **5 MINUTES** | **15 MINUTES** | **1/LOW**

INGREDIENTS

¼ cup steel-cut oats

¼ cup coarse-ground cornmeal

¼ cup buckwheat groats

¼ cup white-rice grits or short-grain white rice

¼ cup whole millet

2½ cups water

½ tsp. kosher salt

½ TB. unsalted butter

½ cup heavy cream

METHOD

1 In a 4-quart (4l) pressure cooker, combine steel-cut oats, coarse-ground cornmeal, buckwheat groats, white-rice grits, millet, water, and kosher salt. Set heat to medium (traditional)/high (electric), and bring to a boil.

2 Lock on the lid, and bring pressure to level 1 (traditional)/low (electric). Reduce heat to low, and cook at 1/low for 15 minutes. Remove from (traditional)/turn off (electric) heat, perform a cold water (traditional)/quick (electric) release, and remove the lid.

3 Serve hot with unsalted butter and heavy cream on the side.

> Coarse-ground cornmeal is sometimes called corn grits. Don't confuse it with plain grits, though. They're not the same.

NUTRITION PER SERVING

| Calories: 320 | Sugars: 0g | Protein: 7g | Cholesterol: 45mg |
| Carbohydrates: 44g | Dietary fiber: 5g | Fat: 14g | Sodium: 250mg |

Eggs cooked in a pressure cooker have a **tender, custardlike** texture. Here, they provide a lovely foundation for the **Gruyère cheese, onion,** and **sausage.**

Sausage, Onion, and Gruyère
Breakfast Casserole

🍴 8 (⅔ CUP) SERVINGS	💨 20 MINUTES	🔥 35 MINUTES	⏲ 2/HIGH

INGREDIENTS

4 slices white bread, cut into 1-in. (2.5cm) cubes (2 cups)

1½ cups breakfast sausage, cooked and crumbled

2 cups grated Gruyère cheese

2 medium green onions, chopped (¼ cup)

1 tsp. unsalted butter

1 small yellow onion, diced small (½ cup)

6 large eggs, beaten

1 cup whole milk

1 TB. Dijon mustard

1 tsp. kosher salt

¼ tsp. freshly ground black pepper

METHOD

1 Add a trivet to a 6-quart (5.5l) pressure cooker, and fill with the minimum amount of water allowed for your cooker. Grease an 8- or 9-inch (20 or 23cm) cake pan (whatever fits in your cooker with space at the edges).

2 In a large bowl, combine white bread, breakfast sausage, Gruyère cheese, and green onions.

3 In a small sauté pan over medium heat, melt unsalted butter. Add yellow onion, and cook for about 5 minutes or until onion is soft. Transfer onion to the bowl, toss to combine, and spread mixture in the cake pan.

4 In the same bowl, whisk together eggs, whole milk, Dijon mustard, kosher salt, and black pepper. Pour eggs over bread, and set aside for 10 minutes.

5 Cover the pan tightly with aluminum foil, and place in the pressure cooker. Set heat to medium (traditional)/high (electric), and bring to a boil.

6 Lock on the lid, bring pressure to level 2 (traditional)/high (electric), and cook for 35 minutes. Remove from (traditional)/turn off (electric) heat, perform a natural release, and remove the lid.

7 Lift casserole out of the cooker, uncover, and serve.

NUTRITION PER SERVING

Calories: **310**	Sugars: **2g**	Protein: **21g**	Cholesterol: **225mg**
Carbohydrates: **8g**	Dietary fiber: **0g**	Fat: **22g**	Sodium: **710mg**

Quinoa is surprisingly **nice and nutty,** and the addition of **honey** and **raisins** makes this a **lovely breakfast treat.**

Honey, Raisin, and Quinoa
Breakfast Risotto

4 (⅔ CUP) SERVINGS	5 MINUTES	8 MINUTES	2/HIGH

INGREDIENTS

1 cup quinoa, rinsed

2 cups water

½ tsp. kosher salt

2 TB. unsalted butter

½ cup raisins

2 tsp. honey

½ cup whole milk

2 TB. heavy cream (optional)

METHOD

1 In a 4-quart (4l) pressure cooker set to medium-high (traditional)/high (electric) heat, combine quinoa, water, and kosher salt. Bring to a boil.

2 Lock on the lid, and bring pressure to level 2 (traditional)/high (electric). Reduce heat to low, and cook at 2/high for 8 minutes. Remove from (traditional)/turn off (electric) heat, perform a cold water (traditional)/quick (electric) release, and remove the lid.

3 Stir in unsalted butter and raisins. Add honey, whole milk, and heavy cream (if using), and stir. If risotto is too thick, add more milk 2 tablespoons at a time. Taste and season with salt as necessary, and serve.

Instead of raisins, you can use dried blueberries.

NUTRITION PER SERVING

Calories: 240	Sugars: 7g	Protein: 7g	Cholesterol: 20mg
Carbohydrates: 32g	Dietary fiber: 3g	Fat: 9g	Sodium: 260mg

This **smoky spread** is rich, satisfying, and **great for brunch**. Although the recipe isn't hard, it is a bit time-consuming, so be patient and don't rush it.

Bacon **Jam**

| 24 (1 TABLESPOON) SERVINGS | 1 HOUR, 5 MINUTES | 12 MINUTES | 2/HIGH |

INGREDIENTS

1 TB. vegetable oil

2 medium yellow onions, diced (1½ cups)

¼ tsp. kosher salt

⅛ tsp. freshly ground black pepper

1 lb. (450g) hickory-smoked bacon, minced

½ cup water

1 TB. brown sugar

2 TB. cider vinegar

2 TB. pure maple syrup

METHOD

1 In a 4-quart (4l) pressure cooker set to medium-high (traditional)/high (electric) heat, heat vegetable oil. When hot, add yellow onions, and sauté for 10 minutes or until onions wilt. Reduce heat to medium-low (traditional)/low (electric), season with kosher salt and black pepper, and cook for about 30 minutes or until onions are very brown.

2 Add bacon, and slowly render fat, allowing it to become crisp.

3 Add water, and bring to a boil.

4 Lock on the lid, bring pressure to level 2 (traditional)/high (electric), and cook for 12 minutes. Remove from (traditional)/turn off (electric) heat, perform a cold water (traditional)/quick (electric) release, and remove the lid.

5 Drain off ½ of liquid. Return jam to medium-low/low heat, and simmer for 10 minutes or until liquid has evaporated.

6 Cook, stirring constantly, for 30 minutes or until jam all falls apart and turns brown.

7 Add brown sugar, cider vinegar, and maple syrup, and cook for 10 minutes or until liquid is absorbed.

8 Serve hot. Refrigerate leftovers in an airtight jar for up to 2 weeks, and warm before serving.

NUTRITION PER SERVING

| Calories: 100 | Sugars: 2g | Protein: 2g | Cholesterol: 15mg |
| Carbohydrates: 2g | Dietary fiber: 0g | Fat: 9g | Sodium: 180mg |

appetizers

Bean dips cooked from dried beans in your pressure cooker are far superior to those made from canned beans, and the smooth and creamy texture a pressure cooker produces isn't possible with traditional cooking methods. It's also ideal for other creamy dips, smooth pâtés, and savory cheesecakes.

The **piquant flavor** of deviled eggs is always a **party pleaser.** Pressure cooked eggs peel easily and perfectly every time, ensuring a **lovely finished dish.**

Classic **Deviled Eggs**

5 (1 EGG) SERVINGS	30 MINUTES	6 MINUTES	2/HIGH

INGREDIENTS

8 large eggs, at room temperature

¾ TB. bread-and-butter pickle juice, or apple cider vinegar

¼ cup mayonnaise

2 tsp. Dijon mustard

½ tsp. kosher salt

2 red or green serrano chiles, sliced into thin rings

1 TB. fresh chives, sliced thin

10 small celery leaves

Freshly ground black pepper

METHOD

1 Add a trivet to the bottom of a 4-quart (4l) pressure cooker. Equally space 8 bottle caps on the trivet, flared side up, and stand 1 egg in each cup, fat end down. Add enough water to the pressure cooker to reach the bottom of the trivet, set heat to medium-high (traditional)/high (electric), and bring to a hard boil.

2 Lock on the lid, bring pressure to level 2 (traditional)/high (electric), and cook for 6 minutes. Remove from (traditional)/turn off (electric) heat, perform a cold water (traditional)/ quick (electric) release, and remove the lid.

3 Run cold water over eggs until they're cool enough to handle, and remove from the pressure cooker. Peel eggs, rinse, and cut in half.

4 Transfer yolks to a medium bowl, and mash with a fork. Add bread-and-butter pickle juice, mayonnaise, Dijon mustard, and kosher salt, and blend to a smooth paste.

5 Spoon yolk mixture back into 10 egg white halves (you'll have a few halves left over). To serve, garnish with serrano chiles, chives, and celery leaves, and season with black pepper. Refrigerate leftovers for up to 3 days.

> If you have a pastry bag, you can pipe the yolk mixture back into the whites. Use a small bag fitted with a star tip.

NUTRITION PER SERVING

Calories: 190	Sugars: 0g	Protein: 10g	Cholesterol: 350mg
Carbohydrates: 2g	Dietary fiber: 0g	Fat: 16g	Sodium: 420mg

Garlic, rosemary, and **Parmesan cheese** star in this dip. Cooking the beans in your pressure cooker yields a **creamier texture** and a **shorter cook time.**

Garlicky **White Bean** and **Parmesan** Dip

10 (¼ CUP) SERVINGS	15 MINUTES + SOAK TIME	8 MINUTES	2/HIGH

INGREDIENTS

1 cup dried cannellini beans, washed, picked over, soaked overnight, and drained

Water

1 tsp. kosher salt

6 cloves garlic

1½ tsp. dried rosemary

¼ tsp. freshly ground black pepper

¼ cup grated Parmesan cheese

1 TB. extra-virgin olive oil

METHOD

1 In a 4-quart (4l) pressure cooker, place cannellini beans. Add enough water to cover by ½ inch (1.25cm), and stir in kosher salt, garlic, rosemary, and black pepper. Set heat to medium-high (traditional)/ high (electric), and bring to a boil.

2 Lock on the lid, and bring pressure to level 2 (traditional)/high (electric). Reduce heat to low, and cook at 2/high for 8 minutes. Remove from (traditional)/turn off (electric) heat, perform a cold water (traditional)/quick (electric) release, and remove the lid.

3 Drain beans, and transfer to a food processor fitted with a metal chopping blade. Add Parmesan cheese, and pulse for 20 seconds or until dip is smooth and creamy. If dip seems too thick, add extra-virgin olive oil and pulse again until blended.

4 Transfer dip to a bowl, and serve warm with pita bread or tortilla chips or as a side dish with roasted meats.

If you're eating Paleo, this recipe fits that diet's requirements.

NUTRITION PER SERVING

Calories: 80	Sugars: 0g	Protein: 5g	Cholesterol: 0mg
Carbohydrates: 11g	Dietary fiber: 3g	Fat: 2g	Sodium: 230mg

This hummus is a lovely **change in color and flavor** from chickpea versions. The beet adds a **sweetness,** and the cashews yield a **nutty creaminess.**

Red Beet **Hummus**

6 (¼ CUP) SERVINGS	10 MINUTES	22 MINUTES	2/HIGH

INGREDIENTS

1 large beet

¾ cup raw cashews

1½ TB. water

½ tsp. crushed cumin

1 TB. freshly squeezed lemon juice

½ tsp. kosher salt

2 tsp. extra-virgin olive oil

METHOD

1 Add a steamer basket to a 4-quart (4l) pressure cooker, add the minimum amount of water allowed for your cooker. Add beet to the basket, set heat to medium-high (traditional)/high (electric), and bring to a boil.

2 Lock on the lid, and bring pressure to level 2 (traditional)/high (electric). Reduce heat to low, and cook at 2/high for 12 minutes. Remove from (traditional)/turn off (electric) heat, and let beet sit for 10 minutes. Perform a natural release, and remove the lid.

3 Meanwhile, in a food processor fitted with a metal chopping blade, pulse together cashews and water to a semismooth paste.

4 Test beet for doneness by inserting a paring knife into middle of beet. The knife should easily glide into center of beet. If not, lock on the lid again, and let beet sit in the closed cooker for 10 more minutes.

5 Remove beet from the pressure cooker, peel it, and cut it into quarters. Add to cashew paste along with cumin, lemon juice, kosher salt, and extra-virgin olive oil. Process for 30 seconds or until hummus becomes smooth and creamy.

6 Transfer hummus to a bowl, and serve with your favorite vegetables, chips, or flatbreads.

NUTRITION PER SERVING

Calories: **157**	Sugars: **3g**	Protein: **4g**	Cholesterol: **0mg**
Carbohydrates: **9g**	Dietary fiber: **2g**	Fat: **13g**	Sodium: **212mg**

Using **hot, fresh-cooked chickpeas** instead of canned gives your hummus a **smoother flavor** that's so worth the effort.

Middle Eastern **Hummus**

8 (¼ CUP) SERVINGS	30 MINUTES + SOAK TIME	11 MINUTES	2/HIGH

INGREDIENTS

1 cup dried chickpeas, washed, picked over, soaked overnight, and drained

Water

1 tsp. kosher salt

2 TB. tahini

3 TB. freshly squeezed lemon juice

1 clove garlic, minced

⅓ cup extra-virgin olive oil

¼ tsp. dried sumac or paprika

METHOD

1 In a 4-quart (4l) pressure cooker, place chickpeas. Add just enough water to cover by 1 inch (2.5cm), and season with ½ teaspoon kosher salt. Set heat to medium-high (traditional)/high (electric), and bring to a boil.

2 Lock on the lid, bring pressure to level 2 (traditional)/high (electric), and cook for 11 minutes. Remove from (traditional)/turn off (electric) heat, perform a cold water (traditional)/quick (electric) release, and remove the lid.

3 Reserve ½ cup cooking liquid, and pour chickpeas into a strainer to drain. Transfer chickpeas to a food processor fitted with a metal chopping blade, and add tahini, lemon juice, garlic, and remaining ½ teaspoon kosher salt. Pulse for 30 seconds or until chickpeas start to break up.

4 Add 2 tablespoons cooking liquid, pulse again, and with the machine running, drizzle in extra-virgin olive oil through the feed tube until hummus reaches a smooth consistency. If it's too thick, add water 1 tablespoon at a time. If it seems dry, add more olive oil 1 tablespoon at a time. Taste, add more salt if necessary, and pulse again for 30 seconds or until smooth.

5 Transfer hummus to a bowl, and serve topped with a drizzle of olive oil and sprinkled with sumac alongside your favorite vegetables, crackers, or chips.

NUTRITION PER SERVING

Calories: 160	Sugars: 2g	Protein: 6g	Cholesterol: 0mg
Carbohydrates: 18g	Dietary fiber: 7g	Fat: 12g	Sodium: 250mg

This is a lovely **appetizer**. It also makes a **wonderful sandwich spread** and is a perfect **sausage substitute** for meatless breakfasts.

Lentil **Pâté**

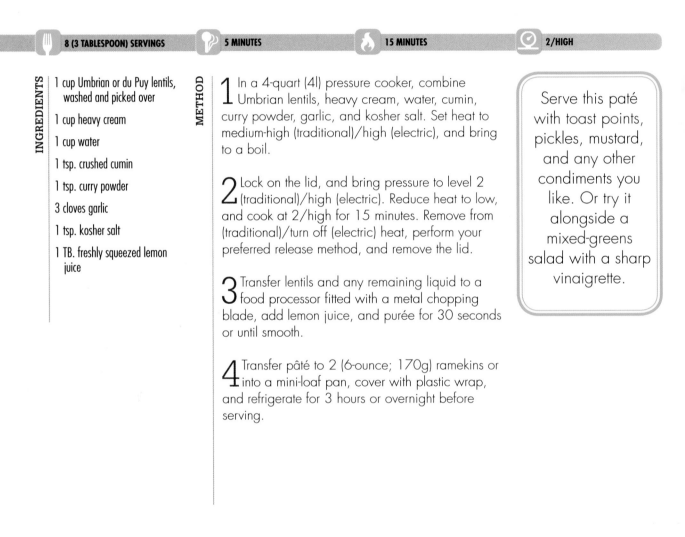

8 (3 TABLESPOON) SERVINGS | **5 MINUTES** | **15 MINUTES** | **2/HIGH**

INGREDIENTS

1 cup Umbrian or du Puy lentils, washed and picked over

1 cup heavy cream

1 cup water

1 tsp. crushed cumin

1 tsp. curry powder

3 cloves garlic

1 tsp. kosher salt

1 TB. freshly squeezed lemon juice

METHOD

1 In a 4-quart (4l) pressure cooker, combine Umbrian lentils, heavy cream, water, cumin, curry powder, garlic, and kosher salt. Set heat to medium-high (traditional)/high (electric), and bring to a boil.

2 Lock on the lid, and bring pressure to level 2 (traditional)/high (electric). Reduce heat to low, and cook at 2/high for 15 minutes. Remove from (traditional)/turn off (electric) heat, perform your preferred release method, and remove the lid.

3 Transfer lentils and any remaining liquid to a food processor fitted with a metal chopping blade, add lemon juice, and purée for 30 seconds or until smooth.

4 Transfer pâté to 2 (6-ounce; 170g) ramekins or into a mini-loaf pan, cover with plastic wrap, and refrigerate for 3 hours or overnight before serving.

Serve this pâté with toast points, pickles, mustard, and any other condiments you like. Or try it alongside a mixed-greens salad with a sharp vinaigrette.

NUTRITION PER SERVING

Calories: **180**	Sugars: **1g**	Protein: **6g**	Cholesterol: **40mg**
Carbohydrates: **15g**	Dietary fiber: **4g**	Fat: **12g**	Sodium: **250mg**

This **sophisticated appetizer** comes together **easily** and **cooks fast.** To really take it over the top, give it a **heavy sprinkle of caviar** before serving.

Savory Smoked **Salmon Cheesecake**

| 12 (⅔ CUP) SERVINGS | 40 MINUTES + COOL TIME | 35 MINUTES | 2/HIGH |

INGREDIENTS

20 saltine crackers

¾ cup grated Parmesan cheese

2 TB. unsalted butter, softened

1 lb. (450g) cream cheese

2 large eggs

1 tsp. grated garlic

1 tsp. grated shallot

¾ tsp. Old Bay seasoning

8 oz. (225g) cured smoked salmon, minced

1 TB. fresh flat-leaf parsley

1 small cucumber, thinly sliced (⅓ cup)

1 TB. minced shallot

1 TB. nonpareil capers, minced

METHOD

1 Butter an 8-inch (20cm) springform pan.

2 In a food processor fitted with a metal chopping blade, pulse saltine crackers, Parmesan cheese, and unsalted butter to a fine crumb. Transfer crust to the pan, and press in an even layer across the bottom and halfway up the sides.

3 In a large bowl, and using an electric mixer on low, blend cream cheese, eggs, garlic, grated shallot, and Old Bay seasoning. Add salmon and flat-leaf parsley, and mix well. Spread filling over crust, smooth the top, and cover with aluminum foil.

4 Add a trivet to the bottom of a 8-quart (7.5l) pressure cooker, and add 1 inch (2.5cm) water. Add the springform pan to the cooker, set heat to medium-high (traditional)/high (electric), and bring to a boil.

5 Lock on the lid, and bring pressure to level 2 (traditional)/high (electric). Reduce heat to low, and cook at 2/high for 35 minutes. Turn off heat, let cake sit for 20 minutes, and remove the lid.

6 Lift out the pan from the cooker, and remove the foil. Give cake a gentle shake; if it jiggles a lot, re-cover, return to the cooker, cook at level 2/high for 10 minutes, and let sit in the cooker for 20 minutes.

7 Refrigerate for 3 hours or until cool. Cover the pan tightly with plastic wrap so it doesn't touch cake, and refrigerate overnight.

8 Remove cake from the pan. Garnish with cucumbers, minced shallot, and capers, and serve with crackers and breads.

NUTRITION PER SERVING

| Calories: 270 | Sugars: 2g | Protein: 17g | Cholesterol: 115mg |
| Carbohydrates: 6g | Dietary fiber: 0g | Fat: 20g | Sodium: 310mg |

salads

With a pressure cooker, you can take salads beyond lettuce. Many of the ancient grains available today form the basis of new and exciting cooked salads, and your pressure cooker makes quick work of these grains. Your favorite classic salads are here, too.

This salad is **creamy, meaty,** and **filling.** The dressing adds the right amount of **tartness** to keep the other ingredients from being cloying.

Tuna Salad with Chickpeas

4 (¾ CUP) SERVINGS	30 MINUTES + SOAK TIME	12 MINUTES	2/HIGH

INGREDIENTS

- 1 cup dried chickpeas, washed, picked over, soaked overnight or quick soaked, and drained
- 1 tsp. kosher salt
- Water
- 1 medium shallot, peeled and minced (2 TB.)
- 1½ TB. fresh flat-leaf parsley, minced
- 1 TB. red wine vinegar
- ¼ tsp. freshly ground black pepper
- 2 (5-oz.; 140g) cans tuna packed in olive oil
- 2 TB. extra-virgin olive oil, plus more to taste
- 8 leaves romaine or Bibb lettuce

METHOD

1 In a 4-quart (4l) pressure cooker, combine chickpeas, kosher salt, and enough water to cover chickpeas by ½ inch (1.25cm). Set heat to medium-high (traditional)/high (electric), and bring to a boil.

2 Lock on the lid, bring pressure to level 2 (traditional)/high (electric), and cook for 12 minutes. Remove from (traditional)/turn off (electric) heat, perform a natural release, and remove the lid.

3 Drain chickpeas into a large bowl, and cool for 5 minutes.

4 Add shallot, flat-leaf parsley, and red wine vinegar, and stir to combine. Taste, season with more kosher salt and black pepper as necessary, and stir.

5 Pour tuna and packing olive oil into the bowl, and gently break up tuna but leave it chunky. Drizzle with extra-virgin olive oil, and gently turn tuna into mixture until distributed. Taste, and adjust seasonings as necessary.

6 Place 2 romaine leaves on each plate, spoon tuna and chickpeas over top, and serve.

NUTRITION PER SERVING

Calories: 330	Sugars: 4g	Protein: 30g	Cholesterol: 45mg
Carbohydrates: 35g	Dietary fiber: 14g	Fat: 17g	Sodium: 920mg

For this delightful **luncheon salad,** I like to use a whole chicken and take advantage of the combination of **light** and **dark meat.**

Chicken Salad Deluxe

🍴 4 (1 CUP) SERVINGS	🍵 35 MINUTES	🔥 20 MINUTES	⏲ 2/HIGH

INGREDIENTS

1 cup water

1½ tsp. kosher salt

1 (2½-lb.; 1.25kg) whole chicken

1½ cups fresh green beans, trimmed

⅔ cup mayonnaise

1½ tsp. Dijon mustard

1 tsp. freshly squeezed lemon juice

3 medium radishes, thinly sliced (½ cup)

1 large carrot, peeled and coarsely grated (¾ cup)

1 TB. fresh chives, minced

⅛ tsp. freshly ground black pepper

8 Bibb lettuce leaves

METHOD

1 In a 6-quart (5.5l) pressure cooker, combine water and ½ teaspoon kosher salt. Add chicken, set heat to medium-high (traditional)/high (electric), and bring to a boil.

2 Lock on the lid, bring pressure to level 2 (traditional)/high (electric), and cook for 15 minutes. Remove from (traditional)/turn off (electric) heat, perform a cold water (traditional)/quick (electric) release, and remove the lid.

3 Add green beans, lock on the lid, and steam green beans for about 5 minutes or until tender.

4 Transfer chicken to a rimmed baking sheet to cool. Remove green beans from the pot, and drain. (Save broth for another use.)

5 Remove skin from chicken, and strip meat from the bones in large, bite-size chunks. Take care to remove all the bones.

6 In a large bowl, combine mayonnaise, Dijon mustard, and lemon juice. Add chicken, radishes, carrot, chives, green beans, remaining 1 teaspoon kosher salt, and black pepper. Stir to combine, and serve.

7 Serve spooned over Bibb lettuce leaves.

NUTRITION PER SERVING

Calories: 450	Sugars: 2g	Protein: 30g	Cholesterol: 110mg
Carbohydrates: 5g	Dietary fiber: 2g	Fat: 34g	Sodium: 880mg

This **cool** egg salad combines **creamy, yolky goodness** with a **celery crunch** and a **mustardy tang.**

Classic **Egg Salad**

🍴 5 (⅓ CUP) SERVINGS	🥄 25 MINUTES	🔥 6 MINUTES	⏲ 2/HIGH

INGREDIENTS

12 large eggs, at room temperature

½ tsp. kosher salt

¼ tsp. freshly ground black pepper

1 medium stalk celery, minced (¼ cup)

1 medium green onion, white parts only, minced (1 TB.)

1½ TB. Dijon mustard

½ cup mayonnaise

METHOD

1 Add a trivet to a 4-quart (4l) pressure cooker, and add enough water to reach the bottom of the trivet.

2 Place eggs in a steamer basket, and add to the pressure cooker. Set heat to medium-high (traditional)/high (electric), and bring to a hard boil.

3 Lock on the lid, bring pressure to level 2 (traditional)/high (electric), and cook for 6 minutes. Remove from (traditional)/turn off (electric) heat, perform a cold water (traditional)/quick (electric) release, and remove the lid.

4 Lift out the steamer basket, and immediately place eggs under cold running water to shock them and make them easier to peel.

5 Peel eggs, place in a large bowl, and mash using a potato masher or the back of a fork.

6 Add kosher salt, black pepper, celery, green onion, Dijon mustard, and mayonnaise. Stir to combine, and serve.

NUTRITION PER SERVING

Calories: 350
Carbohydrates: 2g
Sugars: 1g
Dietary fiber: 0g
Protein: 15g
Fat: 30g
Cholesterol: 515mg
Sodium: 600mg

For a more piquant flavor, add some minced bread-and-butter pickles. Ot try a little curry powder for a more exotic flavor. For a summer-at-the-beach theme, sprinkle a bit of Old Bay seasoning and some capers over the top before serving.

Wheat berries are a **nutritious** ingredient in your diet, and with the addition of **arugula pesto,** they become a **flavorful base** for all types of grain salads.

Wheat Berry Salad with
Arugula Pesto

4 (⅚ CUP) SERVINGS	15 MINUTES	27 MINUTES	2/HIGH

INGREDIENTS

1 cup hard winter wheat berries

3 cups water

¾ tsp. kosher salt

2½ cups arugula leaves

⅓ cup walnuts, coarsely chopped

¼ cup grated Parmesan cheese

¼ tsp. freshly ground black pepper

¼ cup extra-virgin olive oil, plus more as needed

1 cup mixed cherry, plum, and grape tomatoes

4 oz. (110g) fresh mozzarella cheese, shredded

1 TB. fresh chives, minced

METHOD

1 Place wheat berries in a strainer, and rinse well under cold water.

2 Transfer wheat to a 4-quart (4l) pressure cooker, and add water and ½ teaspoon kosher salt. Set heat to medium-high (traditional)/high (electric), and bring to a boil.

3 Lock on the lid, and bring pressure to level 2 (traditional)/high (electric). Reduce heat to low, and cook at 2/high for 27 minutes. Remove from (traditional)/turn off (electric) heat, perform a cold water (traditional)/quick (electric) release, and remove the lid. Set aside to cool.

4 In a food processor fitted with a metal chopping blade, pulse arugula, walnuts, Parmesan cheese, black pepper, and remaining ¼ teaspoon kosher salt. With the food processor running, drizzle extra-virgin olive oil through the feed tube until pesto reaches the consistency of salad dressing.

5 Drain wheat berries, and place in a large bowl. Add ½ of pesto, and stir to combine. Taste, and add more pesto as necessary.

6 Add tomatoes, mozzarella cheese, and chives. Stir gently, and serve.

NUTRITION PER SERVING

Calories: 300	Sugars: 2g	Protein: 18g	Cholesterol: 10mg
Carbohydrates: 39g	Dietary fiber: 7g	Fat: 10g	Sodium: 670mg

Tabbouleh is traditionally made with cracked bulgur wheat. In this version, **farro,** a distant relative of bulgur, makes a **nutty and nutritious** alternative.

Farro **Tabbouleh**

🍴 6 (⅓ CUP) SERVINGS	⏲ 20 MINUTES	🔥 12 MINUTES	⏱ 1/LOW

INGREDIENTS

1 cup farro

5 cups water

1 tsp. kosher salt

½ cup fresh flat-leaf parsley, minced

2 TB. fresh mint, minced

2 TB. fresh chives, minced

½ cup sun-dried tomatoes in oil, drained and chopped

1 cup grape tomatoes, quartered

2½ TB. freshly squeezed lemon juice

2 or 3 TB. extra-virgin olive oil

Freshly ground black pepper

1 cup arugula leaves, rinsed and dried

METHOD

1 Place farro in a strainer, and rinse well under cold water.

2 Transfer farro to a 4-quart (4l) pressure cooker, and add water and kosher salt. Set heat to medium-high (traditional)/high (electric), and bring to a boil.

3 Lock on the lid, and bring pressure to level 1 (traditional)/high (electric). Reduce heat to low, and cook at 1/low for 12 minutes. Remove from (traditional)/turn off (electric) heat, perform a cold water (traditional)/quick (electric) release, and remove the lid.

4 Return farro to the strainer, and cool.

5 In a large bowl, combine cooled farro, flat-leaf parsley, mint, chives, sun-dried tomatoes, grape tomatoes, lemon juice, and extra-virgin olive oil.

6 Taste, and season with more kosher salt and black pepper as necessary. Add arugula, stir, and serve.

> Farro contains more protein, fiber, vitamins, and minerals than bulgur. It also has more fat.

NUTRITION PER SERVING

Calories: **70**	Sugars: **1g**	Protein: **1g**	Cholesterol: **0mg**
Carbohydrates: **5g**	Dietary fiber: **1g**	Fat: **6g**	Sodium: **350mg**

Tart from the **buttermilk** and **herby** from the **dill,** this is homemade potato salad at its finest. It's ideal for family gatherings, potlucks, pitch-ins—and picnics.

Picnic-Style Potato Salad

10 (½ CUP) SERVINGS	30 MINUTES + COOL TIME	5 MINUTES	2/HIGH

INGREDIENTS

10 medium Yukon Gold potatoes, cut in half and then into ½ moons

¾ cup mayonnaise

¼ cup buttermilk

1 TB. Dijon mustard

½ tsp. kosher salt

¼ tsp. freshly ground white pepper

1 medium green onion, minced (1 TB.)

1 TB. fresh flat-leaf parsley

2 tsp. fresh dill, minced

3 large hard-boiled eggs, peeled and sliced thin

METHOD

1 Add a steamer basket to a 4-quart (4l) pressure cooker, and fill with the minimum amount of water allowed for your cooker. Set heat to medium-high (traditional)/high (electric), and bring to a boil.

2 Add Yukon Gold potatoes to the basket.

3 Lock on the lid, and bring pressure to level 2 (traditional)/high (electric). Reduce heat to low, and cook at 2/high for 5 minutes. Remove from (traditional)/turn off (electric) heat, perform a quick release, and remove the lid.

4 Let potatoes steam dry in the cooker for 30 seconds.

5 In a large bowl, whisk together mayonnaise, buttermilk, Dijon mustard, kosher salt, white pepper, green onion, flat-leaf parsley, and dill until smooth.

6 Add potatoes, and stir to coat. Refrigerate for 1 hour or until cool.

7 Stir well, top with hard-boiled egg slices, and serve.

NUTRITION PER SERVING

Calories: 270	Sugars: 3g	Protein: 6g	Cholesterol: 60mg
Carbohydrates: 25g	Dietary fiber: 3g	Fat: 18g	Sodium: 320mg

This hot German-style potato salad—the **perfect side** to **sausage** and **Wiener schnitzel**—uses **rich beef stock** as a thickener for a **lighter** finished dish.

Hot German Potato Salad

8 (½ CUP) SERVINGS	30 MINUTES	5 MINUTES	2/HIGH

INGREDIENTS

- 2 slices smoky bacon, sliced into ¼-in. (.5cm) pieces
- 1 medium yellow onion, thinly sliced (about 1 cup)
- 1 cup homemade or sodium-free beef stock
- 2 lb. (1kg) red potatoes, cut into ½-in. (1.25cm) slices
- ½ tsp. kosher salt
- ¼ tsp. freshly ground black pepper
- 2 TB. fresh flat-leaf parsley, minced
- 3 TB. cider vinegar or to taste

METHOD

1 In a 4-quart (4l) pressure cooker, add bacon. Set heat to medium (traditional)/high (electric), and slowly render fat from bacon, allowing it to become crisp. Transfer bacon to a paper towel–lined plate.

2 Add yellow onion to the cooker, and sauté for about 3 minutes or until wilted. Transfer onion to a bowl, and set aside.

3 Add beef stock to the cooker, add a layer of red potatoes, dot with onions, and season with a pinch of kosher salt and a grind of black pepper. Repeat layering, ending with potatoes. Bring to a boil.

4 Lock on the lid, bring pressure to level 2 (traditional)/high (electric), and cook for 5 minutes. Remove from (traditional)/turn off (electric) heat, perform a cold water (traditional)/quick (electric) release, and remove the lid.

5 Gently transfer potatoes to a large bowl. Add ⅔ of bacon, ½ of flat-leaf parsley, and cider vinegar, and toss to combine.

6 Transfer to a serving bowl, and wet with ½ cup hot broth. Top with remaining bacon and parsley, sprinkle with a little more vinegar, and serve.

NUTRITION PER SERVING

Calories: 120	Sugars: 2g	Protein: 4g	Cholesterol: 5mg
Carbohydrates: 20g	Dietary fiber: 2g	Fat: 3g	Sodium: 180mg

soups, stews, and **chilies**

A pressure cooker excels when it comes to making soups. In no time, you can serve your family steaming bowls of sensational soups, stews, chilies, and chowders with flavors inspired by cuisines from around the world.

All-bean chili is **hearty** and **filling,** but add some roasted corn, butternut squash, yellow corn chips, and **southwestern spices,** and it's so much better.

Roasted Corn and Butternut Squash **Chili**

🍴 8 (1 CUP) SERVINGS	🕐 30 MINUTES + SOAK TIME	🔥 12 MINUTES	⏱ 2/HIGH

INGREDIENTS

1½ TB. vegetable oil

1 large yellow onion, diced small (1 cup)

1 small butternut squash, peeled, seeded, and cut into ½-in. (1.25cm) cubes (2 cups)

1 cup fresh or frozen yellow corn

1 lb. (450g) dried mixed chili beans (pintos, kidney, black, and red), washed, picked over, soaked overnight or quick soaked, and drained

1 tsp. kosher salt

2 TB. dark chili powder

1 TB. ground cumin

1 TB. dried oregano

1 TB. garlic powder

2¼ cups tomato sauce

1 cup water

¼ cup crushed yellow corn tortilla chips

3 medium Fresno chiles, sliced (½ cup)

½ cup fresh cilantro, coarsely chopped

1 cup sour cream

2 cups corn chips

2 cups shredded cheddar cheese

METHOD

1 In a 6-quart (5.5l) pressure cooker set to medium-high (traditional)/high (electric) heat, heat vegetable oil, swirling the cooker to coat.

2 Add yellow onion, and sauté for 5 minutes or until onion begins to soften.

3 Add butternut squash, corn, chili beans, kosher salt, dark chili powder, cumin, oregano, and garlic powder. Cook, stirring, for 1 minute or until spices become fragrant.

4 Add tomato sauce, water, and yellow corn tortilla chips, and bring to a boil.

5 Lock on the lid, bring pressure to level 2 (traditional)/high (electric), and cook for 12 minutes. Remove from (traditional)/turn off (electric) heat, and let chili sit for 5 minutes. Perform a cold water (traditional)/quick (electric) release, and remove the lid.

6 Taste, and adjust kosher salt as necessary. Spoon chili into bowls, and serve with Fresno chiles, cilantro, sour cream, corn chips, and cheddar cheese for topping.

NUTRITION PER SERVING

Calories: 360
Carbohydrates: 53g
Sugars: 7g
Dietary fiber: 14g
Protein: 25g
Fat: 7g
Cholesterol: 5mg
Sodium: 850mg

Either **vegetable** or **mushroom broth** works well in this easy soup and marries with the **shiitakes** and **cannellini beans** to yield deep, wonderful flavors.

White Bean and Shiitake **Soup**

8 (1 CUP) SERVINGS	30 MINUTES + SOAK TIME	12 MINUTES	2/HIGH

INGREDIENTS

3 TB. olive oil

1 large yellow onion, diced small (1½ cups)

1 tsp. kosher salt

¼ tsp. freshly ground black pepper

2 cups shiitake mushrooms, sliced

6 cloves garlic, minced

1 TB. dried rosemary, crushed

1 cup dried cannellini beans, washed, picked over, soaked overnight, and drained

4 cups homemade or sodium-free vegetable or mushroom broth

1 (14.5-oz.; 410g) can chopped tomatoes, with juice

METHOD

1 In a 4-quart (4l) pressure cooker, add olive oil. Set heat to medium (traditional)/high (electric), and heat oil for 20 seconds. Add yellow onion, and sauté for 3 or 4 minutes or until softened.

2 Season with kosher salt and black pepper, add shiitake mushrooms, stir, and sauté for 3 to 5 minutes or until softened.

3 Add garlic and rosemary, and stir. When garlic is fragrant, add cannellini beans and vegetable broth, and bring to a boil.

4 Lock on the lid, and bring pressure to level 2 (traditional)/high (electric). Reduce heat to low, and cook at 2/high for 12 minutes. Remove from (traditional)/turn off (electric) heat, perform a cold water (traditional)/quick (electric) release, and remove the lid.

5 Taste, and season with additional salt and pepper as necessary. Add tomatoes with juice, set heat to low, and cook for 5 minutes.

6 Serve hot.

NUTRITION PER SERVING

Calories: 160	Sugars: 4g	Protein: 7g	Cholesterol: 0mg
Carbohydrates: 21g	Dietary fiber: 5g	Fat: 5g	Sodium: 120mg

Ham and beans is a favorite for many, especially when served with **cornbread.** With your pressure cooker, you can make these **filling beans** in no time.

Saturday Soup **Beans**

| | 8 (1 CUP) SERVINGS | | 20 MINUTES + SOAK TIME | | 41 MINUTES | | 2/HIGH |

INGREDIENTS

2 (8-oz.; 225g) meaty smoked ham hocks

Water

1½ cups dried pinto beans, washed, picked over, soaked overnight, and drained

2 tsp. kosher salt

1 tsp. freshly ground black pepper

1 small red onion, diced small (½ cup)

3 medium green onions, chopped (½ cup)

Hot sauce

METHOD

1 In a 6-quart (5.5l) pressure cooker, place ham hocks. Add enough water to come halfway up hocks, set heat to high (traditional)/high (electric), and bring to a boil.

2 Lock on the lid, and bring pressure to level 2 (traditional)/high (electric). Reduce heat to low, and cook at 2/high for 30 minutes. Remove from (traditional)/turn off (electric) heat, perform a cold water (traditional)/quick (electric) release, and remove the lid.

3 Add pinto beans, and ensure broth covers beans by 1 inch (2.5cm). If it's too low, add water; if it's too high, use a ladle to remove some liquid. Add kosher salt and black pepper, set heat to medium-high (traditional)/high (electric), and bring to a boil.

4 Lock on the lid, and bring pressure to level 2/high. Reduce heat to low, and cook at 2/high for 11 minutes. Remove from/turn off heat, perform a cold water/quick release, and remove the lid.

5 Transfer hocks to a cutting board, and remove and set aside outer skin. Pull or cut meat from hocks, leaving sinew, bones, and fat behind. Chop meat.

6 Using a potato masher, mash some beans to make soup creamy.

7 Return meat to the cooker, stir, taste, and season with kosher salt or black pepper as necessary. Serve hot, with red onion, green onions, and hot sauce for topping.

NUTRITION PER SERVING

Calories: **270**	Sugars: **1g**	Protein: **24g**	Cholesterol: **55mg**
Carbohydrates: **23g**	Dietary fiber: **8g**	Fat: **9g**	Sodium: **520mg**

This **zesty** stew is the perfect balance of **hot** and **sour.** Be aware that the more **tamarind** you add, the **sourer** the dish will be.

Spicy Chickpea Stew with Sour Tomato Curry

6 (⅔ CUP) SERVINGS	30 MINUTES + SOAK TIME	12 MINUTES	2/HIGH

INGREDIENTS

3 TB. olive oil

2 medium yellow onions, julienned (2 cups)

¾ tsp. kosher salt

1 TB. minced garlic

1 (1-in; 2.5cm) piece fresh ginger, peeled and minced (1 TB.)

1 tsp. turmeric

¼ tsp. cayenne (optional)

2 tsp. Madras curry powder

1 tsp. coarsely ground cumin

¼ tsp. freshly ground black pepper

1½ cups dried chickpeas, washed, picked over, soaked overnight, and drained

2 cups tomato sauce

1½ TB. tamarind concentrate mixed with ½ cup water, or 1 TB. brown sugar mixed with 1 TB. freshly squeezed lime juice

1 lb. (450g) cooked spaghetti, hot

⅓ cup fresh cilantro, chopped

2 large green onions, chopped (⅓ cup)

NUTRITION PER SERVING

Calories: 330
Carbohydrates: 66g
Sugars: 9g
Dietary fiber: 17g
Protein: 17g
Fat: 10g
Cholesterol: 0mg
Sodium: 700mg

METHOD

1 In a 4-quart (4l) pressure cooker set to medium-high (traditional)/high (electric) heat, heat olive oil. Add yellow onions and ¼ teaspoon kosher salt, and cook for 5 minutes or until onions begin to sizzle. Reduce to medium (traditional)/high (electric) heat, and cook, stirring occasionally, for 10 minutes or until onions turn dark brown.

2 Stir in garlic, ginger, turmeric, cayenne (if using), Madras curry powder, cumin, and black pepper, and sauté for about 30 seconds.

3 Stir in chickpeas, tomato sauce, remaining ½ teaspoon kosher salt, and tamarind-water mixture, and bring to a boil.

4 Lock on the lid, and bring pressure to level 2 (traditional)/high (electric). Reduce heat to low, and cook at 2/high for 12 minutes. Remove from (traditional)/turn off (electric) heat, and let sit for 5 minutes. Perform a natural release, and remove the lid.

5 Spoon chickpeas over spaghetti, garnish with cilantro and green onions, and serve.

The addition of **sherry** brings a touch of **elegance** to this otherwise **homey soup** that's inspired by the influence of Spanish cuisine on Cuban food.

Cuban Black Bean Soup
with Sherry

6 (1⅓ CUP) SERVINGS	30 MINUTES + SOAK TIME	11 MINUTES	2/HIGH

INGREDIENTS

3 TB. olive oil

2 to 4 slices bacon, diced small

1 large yellow onion, diced small (1½ cups)

4 medium stalks celery, chopped (¾ cup)

2 ancho chiles, diced small (¾ cup)

2 TB. minced garlic

1 TB. dried oregano

1 TB. crushed cumin

3 bay leaves

2 TB. dry sherry

8 oz. (225g) dried black beans, washed, picked over, soaked overnight, and drained

1 cup tomato sauce

¼ cup fresh cilantro, chopped

Water

1 small red onion, minced (½ cup)

¾ cup sour cream

METHOD

1 In a 4-quart (4l) pressure cooker set to medium (traditional)/high (electric) heat, heat olive oil. Add bacon, yellow onion, celery, and ancho chiles, and sauté for about 4 minutes or until softened.

2 Stir in garlic, oregano, cumin, and bay leaves, and cook for 20 seconds or until garlic becomes fragrant.

3 Add sherry, and cook for 15 seconds to burn off alcohol.

4 Add black beans, tomato sauce, and ½ of cilantro. Add water to cover beans by 1 inch (2.5cm), stir to combine, and bring to a boil.

5 Lock on the lid, bring pressure to level 2 (traditional)/high (electric), and cook for 11 minutes. Remove from (traditional)/turn off (electric) heat, perform a cold water (traditional)/quick (electric) release, and remove the lid.

6 Remove bay leaves. Spoon soup into bowls, and serve with red onion, sour cream, and remaining cilantro for topping.

NUTRITION PER SERVING

Calories: **440**

Carbohydrates: **40g**

Sugars: **5g**

Dietary fiber: **8g**

Protein: **14g**

Fat: **21g**

Cholesterol: **35mg**

Sodium: **840mg**

This **rustic chowder** is unbelievable in the summertime, when **sweet corn** is in season. In the off season, you can use frozen corn for an equally lovely result.

Farmhouse **Corn Chowder**

🍴 6 (1½ CUP) SERVINGS	🔪 30 MINUTES	🔥 4 MINUTES	⏲ 2/HIGH

INGREDIENTS

3 thick slices smoky bacon, cut into ¼-in. (.5cm) pieces

1 TB. unsalted butter

1 large yellow onion, diced medium (1 cup)

3 medium stalks celery, diced medium (½ cup)

1 medium green bell pepper, ribs and seeds removed, and diced medium (½ cup)

1 TB. minced garlic

1 tsp. kosher salt

¼ tsp. freshly ground black pepper

4 medium russet potatoes, peeled and diced medium (2 cups)

2 ears sweet corn, husked and kernels cut from cob (1 cup), or 1 cup frozen corn

5 cups homemade or sodium-free chicken stock

2 tsp. fresh chives, minced

2 tsp. fresh flat-leaf parsley, minced

METHOD

1 In a 4-quart (4l) pressure cooker, add bacon. Set heat to medium (traditional)/high (electric), and slowly render fat from bacon, allowing it to become crisp. Transfer bacon to a paper towel–lined plate. Pour off all but 1 tablespoon grease.

2 Add unsalted butter to the cooker, and melt. Add yellow onion, celery, green bell pepper, garlic, ½ teaspoon kosher salt, and black pepper, and sauté for about 3 or 4 minutes or until soft.

3 Add russet potatoes, sweet corn, chicken stock, and remaining ½ teaspoon kosher salt, and bring liquid to a boil.

4 Lock on the lid, bring pressure to level 2 (traditional)/high (electric), and cook for 4 minutes. Remove from (traditional)/turn off (electric) heat, perform a cold water (traditional)/quick (electric) release, and remove the lid.

5 Stir in chives, flat-leaf parsley, and ½ of bacon. Taste, and add more salt as necessary. Serve garnished with remaining bacon.

NUTRITION PER SERVING

Calories: 280

Carbohydrates: 33g

Sugars: 4g

Dietary fiber: 3g

Protein: 11g

Fat: 12g

Cholesterol: 40mg

Sodium: 610mg

This **classic French bistro** soup is **smooth, creamy,** and **comforting.** Make it a bit more elegant by **puréeing** it after it's cooked and has cooled a bit.

French Potato and Leek **Soup**

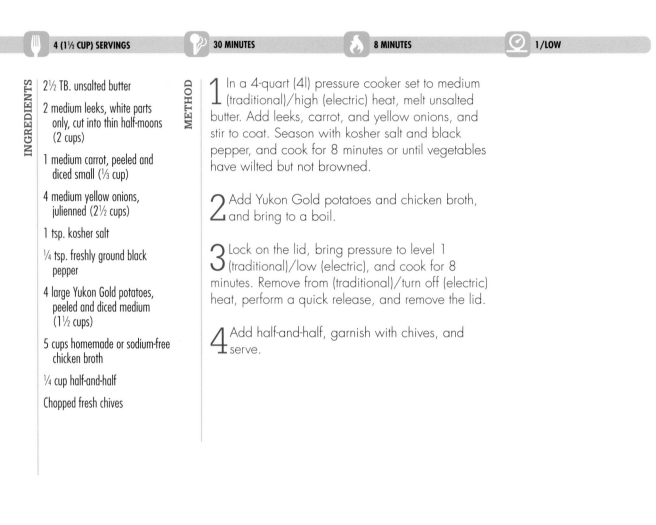

| 4 (1½ CUP) SERVINGS | 30 MINUTES | 8 MINUTES | 1/LOW |

INGREDIENTS

2½ TB. unsalted butter

2 medium leeks, white parts only, cut into thin half-moons (2 cups)

1 medium carrot, peeled and diced small (⅓ cup)

4 medium yellow onions, julienned (2½ cups)

1 tsp. kosher salt

¼ tsp. freshly ground black pepper

4 large Yukon Gold potatoes, peeled and diced medium (1½ cups)

5 cups homemade or sodium-free chicken broth

¼ cup half-and-half

Chopped fresh chives

METHOD

1 In a 4-quart (4l) pressure cooker set to medium (traditional)/high (electric) heat, melt unsalted butter. Add leeks, carrot, and yellow onions, and stir to coat. Season with kosher salt and black pepper, and cook for 8 minutes or until vegetables have wilted but not browned.

2 Add Yukon Gold potatoes and chicken broth, and bring to a boil.

3 Lock on the lid, bring pressure to level 1 (traditional)/low (electric), and cook for 8 minutes. Remove from (traditional)/turn off (electric) heat, perform a quick release, and remove the lid.

4 Add half-and-half, garnish with chives, and serve.

NUTRITION PER SERVING

| Calories: 270 | Sugars: 6g | Protein: 11g | Cholesterol: 55mg |
| Carbohydrates: 34g | Dietary fiber: 4g | Fat: 11g | Sodium: 670mg |

Slightly exotic and spicy but not hot, this soup is influenced mostly by the flavors of Indian cuisine but mixes in a little bit of everything.

Indian Carrot and Lentil **Soup**

4 (1½ CUP) SERVINGS	25 MINUTES	12 MINUTES	1/LOW

INGREDIENTS

1 TB. olive oil

6 medium carrots, peeled and chopped (1½ cups)

1 medium yellow onion, halved and thinly sliced (1 cup)

1 tsp. kosher salt

½ cup red (pink) lentils

¼ cup jasmine rice

1 (1-in; 2.5cm) piece fresh ginger, peeled and minced (1 TB.)

1½ tsp. Thai red curry paste

1 tsp. curry powder

4 cups homemade or sodium-free chicken stock

½ cup coconut milk

METHOD

1 In a 4-quart (4l) pressure cooker set to medium-high (traditional)/high (electric) heat, heat olive oil. Add carrots, yellow onion, and kosher salt, and sauté for about 8 minutes or until golden.

2 Add red lentils, jasmine rice, ginger, Thai red curry paste, and curry powder, and stir to combine. When spices sizzle and pop and become fragrant, add chicken stock and bring to a boil.

3 Lock on the lid, and bring pressure to level 1 (traditional)/low (electric). Reduce heat to low, and cook at 1/low for 12 minutes. Remove from (traditional)/turn off (electric) heat, perform a cold water (traditional)/quick (electric) release, and remove the lid.

4 Add coconut milk, stir to blend, and serve hot.

For a smoother soup, purée it in a blender after cooling it for a while first. Never purée a hot soup in a blender. Cool it first, blend it, return it to the pot, and reheat before serving.

NUTRITION PER SERVING

Calories: 280	Sugars: 5g	Protein: 12g	Cholesterol: 25mg
Carbohydrates: 33g	Dietary fiber: 6g	Fat: 12g	Sodium: 670mg

Traditionally, this soup is puréed to a **smooth finish.** This version is **rustic and hearty,** and the **ham** added at the end brings a new flavor to the final soup.

Rustic Split-Pea **Soup**

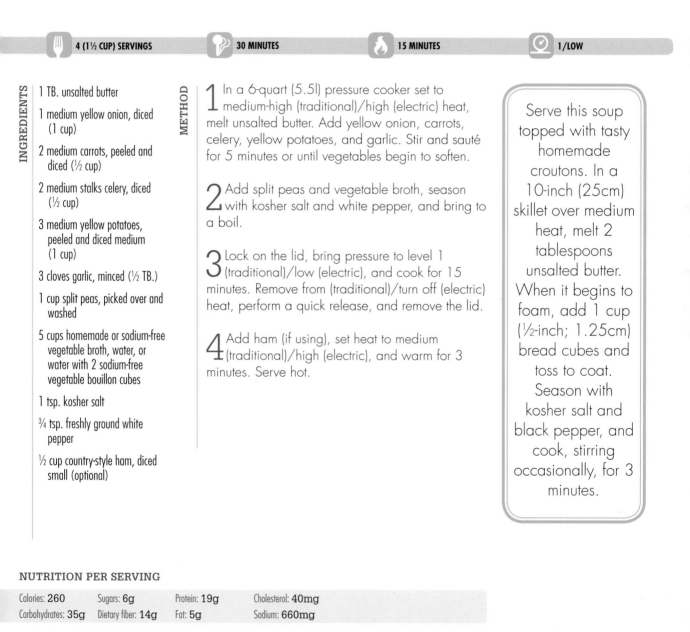

	4 (1½ CUP) SERVINGS		30 MINUTES		15 MINUTES		1/LOW

INGREDIENTS

1 TB. unsalted butter

1 medium yellow onion, diced (1 cup)

2 medium carrots, peeled and diced (½ cup)

2 medium stalks celery, diced (½ cup)

3 medium yellow potatoes, peeled and diced medium (1 cup)

3 cloves garlic, minced (½ TB.)

1 cup split peas, picked over and washed

5 cups homemade or sodium-free vegetable broth, water, or water with 2 sodium-free vegetable bouillon cubes

1 tsp. kosher salt

¾ tsp. freshly ground white pepper

½ cup country-style ham, diced small (optional)

METHOD

1 In a 6-quart (5.5l) pressure cooker set to medium-high (traditional)/high (electric) heat, melt unsalted butter. Add yellow onion, carrots, celery, yellow potatoes, and garlic. Stir and sauté for 5 minutes or until vegetables begin to soften.

2 Add split peas and vegetable broth, season with kosher salt and white pepper, and bring to a boil.

3 Lock on the lid, bring pressure to level 1 (traditional)/low (electric), and cook for 15 minutes. Remove from (traditional)/turn off (electric) heat, perform a quick release, and remove the lid.

4 Add ham (if using), set heat to medium (traditional)/high (electric), and warm for 3 minutes. Serve hot.

Serve this soup topped with tasty homemade croutons. In a 10-inch (25cm) skillet over medium heat, melt 2 tablespoons unsalted butter. When it begins to foam, add 1 cup (½-inch; 1.25cm) bread cubes and toss to coat. Season with kosher salt and black pepper, and cook, stirring occasionally, for 3 minutes.

NUTRITION PER SERVING

Calories: 260	Sugars: 6g	Protein: 19g	Cholesterol: 40mg
Carbohydrates: 35g	Dietary fiber: 14g	Fat: 5g	Sodium: 660mg

Easy-to-purée butternut squash is an **ideal, adaptable** base for all kinds of flavor additions.

Curried Butternut Squash **Soup**

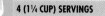

4 (1¼ CUP) SERVINGS	30 MINUTES	8 MINUTES	2/HIGH

INGREDIENTS

1 TB. vegetable oil

1 medium yellow onion, thinly sliced (1 cup)

3 cloves garlic

1½ TB. curry powder

1 TB. Thai red curry paste

2 cups homemade or sodium-free vegetable stock, or 2 cups water with 2 cubes sodium-free vegetable bouillon

½ tsp. kosher salt

2 medium butternut squash, peeled, seeded, and cut into 1-in. (2.5cm) cubes (2½ cups)

1 medium carrot, peeled and diced large (⅔ cup)

1 medium roma tomato, cored and diced medium

1 serrano chile, thinly sliced

1 TB. fresh cilantro, minced

2 TB. plain yogurt

METHOD

1 In a 4-quart (4l) pressure cooker set to medium (traditional)/high (electric) heat, heat vegetable oil. Add yellow onion, and sauté for about 10 minutes or until onion is golden.

2 Add garlic, curry powder, and Thai red curry paste, and cook, stirring, for 30 seconds minutes or until fragrant.

3 Add vegetable stock, kosher salt, butternut squash, and carrot, and bring to a boil.

4 Lock on the lid, and bring pressure to level 2 (traditional)/high (electric). Reduce heat to low, and cook at 2/high for 8 minutes. Remove from (traditional)/turn off (electric) heat, perform a cold water (traditional)/quick (electric) release, and remove the lid.

5 Let soup cool, transfer to a blender or a food processor fitted with a metal chopping blade, and purée until smooth. Return soup to the pressure cooker, set heat to medium/high, and warm.

6 Meanwhile, in a small bowl, combine roma tomato, serrano chile, cilantro, and yogurt.

7 Divide warmed soup among 4 bowls, top each with 1 dollop tomato raita, and serve.

NUTRITION PER SERVING

Calories: **120**	Sugars: **7g**	Protein: **2g**	Cholesterol: **0mg**
Carbohydrates: **22g**	Dietary fiber: **4g**	Fat: **4g**	Sodium: **340mg**

This **hearty** soup delivers **warmth** and **comfort** in every bowl. The **deep, earthy flavor** of mushrooms combines nicely with the **nutty barley.**

Mushroom Barley **Soup**

6 (1¼ CUP) SERVINGS	30 MINUTES	10 MINUTES	2/HIGH

INGREDIENTS

3 TB. unsalted butter

8 oz. (225g) cremini or white mushrooms, brushed clean and thinly sliced (3 cups)

1 tsp. kosher salt

¼ tsp. freshly ground black pepper

1 large yellow onion, diced medium (1½ cups)

3 medium carrots, peeled and sliced into rounds (¾ cup)

4 medium stalks celery, sliced into thin half-moons (¾ cup)

1 TB. minced garlic

½ cup pearl barley

½ tsp. dried thyme

4 cups homemade or sodium-free beef, chicken, or vegetable stock

1 TB. fresh flat-leaf parsley, minced

METHOD

1 In a 4-quart (4l) pressure cooker set to medium-high (traditional)/high (electric) heat, melt unsalted butter. Add cremini mushrooms, kosher salt, and black pepper, and sauté for about 4 minutes or until soft.

2 Add yellow onion, carrots, celery, and garlic, and sauté for 30 seconds or until aromatic.

3 Add pearl barley, and stir to coat with butter. Add thyme and beef stock, and bring to a boil.

4 Lock on the lid, bring pressure to level 2 (traditional)/high (electric), and cook for 10 minutes. Remove from (traditional)/turn off (electric) heat, perform a cold water (traditional)/quick (electric) release, and remove the lid.

5 Stir in flat-leaf parsley, and serve.

For a gluten-free soup, use brown rice or whole-grain white sorghum instead of the barley. For a heartier soup, add some cooked shredded beef.

NUTRITION PER SERVING

Calories: 160	Sugars: 5g	Protein: 4g	Cholesterol: 20mg
Carbohydrates: 22g	Dietary fiber: 5g	Fat: 6g	Sodium: 770mg

This healthy soup is full of **hearty root vegetables.** Your pressure cooker **quickly cooks** these vegetables that usually take longer via traditional methods.

Root Vegetable **Stew**

4 (2 CUP) SERVINGS	30 MINUTES	6 MINUTES	2/HIGH

INGREDIENTS

¼ cup olive oil

1 tsp. fresh rosemary, minced

1 large yellow onion, diced large (1 cup)

1 (3-in.; 7.5cm) celery root, peeled and diced large (1½ cups)

1 medium bulb fennel, trimmed and sliced (¾ cup)

2 large russet potatoes, peeled and diced large (2 cups)

3 medium carrots, peeled and diced large (1 cup)

1 large turnip, peeled and diced large (1 cup)

2 medium parsnips, peeled and diced large (1 cup)

3 cups homemade or sodium-free chicken stock

¾ tsp. kosher salt

¼ tsp. freshly ground black pepper

1 TB. fresh chives, minced

METHOD

1 In a 6-quart (5.5l) pressure cooker set to medium-high (traditional)/high (electric) heat, heat olive oil. Add rosemary, and when it begins to sizzle, immediately add yellow onion and stir. Do not let rosemary burn.

2 Add celery root, fennel, russet potatoes, carrots, turnip, parsnips, chicken stock, kosher salt, and black pepper, and bring to a boil.

3 Lock on the lid, bring pressure to level 2 (traditional)/high (electric), and cook for 6 minutes. Remove from (traditional)/turn off (electric) heat, perform a cold water (traditional)/quick (electric) release, and remove the lid.

4 Garnish with chives, and serve.

NUTRITION PER SERVING

Calories: 340	Sugars: 9g	Protein: 7g	Cholesterol: 5mg
Carbohydrates: 46g	Dietary fiber: 9g	Fat: 15g	Sodium: 970mg

This **lovely purple** soup is nice any time of year. The **fennel seed** in the soup and in the sausage pairs well with the **vegetables, sour cream,** and **lemon.**

Borscht with Italian Sausage

🍴 4 (2 CUP) SERVINGS	🥄 30 MINUTES	🔥 7 MINUTES	⏲ 1/LOW

INGREDIENTS

1½ TB. unsalted butter

8 oz. (225g) Italian sausage

2 medium beets, peeled and cut into ½-in. (1.25cm) cubes (1 cup)

2 medium carrots, peeled and diced small (½ cup)

½ medium head red or green cabbage, cored and thinly shredded (2 cups)

2 tsp. minced garlic

½ tsp. kosher salt

¼ tsp. freshly ground black pepper

1 bay leaf

½ tsp. fennel seed

4 cups homemade or sodium-free beef broth

1 TB. red wine vinegar

1 medium lemon, quartered

½ cup sour cream

METHOD

1 In a 6-quart (5.5l) pressure cooker set to medium-high (traditional)/high (electric) heat, melt unsalted butter. Add Italian sausage, brown for 3 minutes on both sides, and transfer sausage to a plate.

2 Add beets, carrots, red cabbage, and garlic to the pressure cooker, and stir. Season with kosher salt and black pepper, and stir again. Add bay leaf, fennel seed, beef broth, and red wine vinegar, and stir again. Return sausage to the pan, and bring to a boil.

3 Lock on the lid, bring pressure to level 1 (traditional)/low (electric), and cook for 7 minutes. Remove from (traditional)/turn off (electric) heat, perform a cold water (traditional)/quick (electric) release, and remove the lid.

4 Remove bay leaf. Transfer sausage to a cutting board, cut into 1-inch (2.5cm) rounds, and return to the cooker. Taste, and add more kosher salt as necessary, and stir.

5 Divide soup among 4 bowls, and serve with lemon quarters and sour cream on the side.

NUTRITION PER SERVING

Calories: 200

Carbohydrates: 16g

Sugars: 10g

Dietary fiber: 4g

Protein: 8g

Fat: 11g

Cholesterol: 30mg

Sodium: 390mg

This **Italian** soup is based on Italian bread soups that use **leftover bread** as a thickener to make the soup **more filling.**

Ribolleta

🍴 6 (1½ CUP) SERVINGS	🥄 30 MINUTES	🔥 8 MINUTES	⏲ 2/HIGH

INGREDIENTS

4 TB. olive oil, plus more for garnish

¼ lb. (115g) pancetta, diced

1 cup dried cannellini beans, washed, picked over, soaked overnight, and drained

1 medium zucchini, diced large (1 cup)

1 medium yellow onion, diced large (1 cup)

2 medium stalks celery, diced large (⅔ cup)

2 medium carrots, peeled and diced large (⅔ cup)

2 TB. minced garlic

¼ medium head green cabbage, chopped (2 cups)

1 cup canned crushed tomatoes, with juice

½ cup fresh basil, torn

¾ tsp. kosher salt

4 cups homemade or sodium-free chicken stock

4 pieces day-old sourdough bread, cut into ½-in. (1.25cm) cubes (2 cups)

2 cups spinach

½ cup grated Parmesan cheese

¼ tsp. freshly ground black pepper

METHOD

1 In a 6-quart (5.5l) pressure cooker set to medium-high (traditional)/high (electric) heat, heat olive oil. Add pancetta, and slowly render fat from pancetta, allowing it to become crisp.

2 Add cannellini beans, zucchini, yellow onion, celery, carrots, garlic, green cabbage, tomatoes with juice, basil, kosher salt, and chicken stock, and bring to a boil.

3 Lock on the lid, and bring pressure to level 2 (traditional)/high (electric). Reduce heat to low, and cook at 2/high for 8 minutes. Remove from (traditional)/turn off (electric) heat, perform a cold water (traditional)/quick (electric) release, and remove the lid.

4 Return the pressure cooker to medium (traditional)/high (electric) heat, stir in sourdough bread cubes and spinach, and cook for 10 minutes or until bread has dissolved into broth and spinach has wilted.

5 Serve sprinkled with Parmesan cheese, a drizzle of olive oil, and freshly ground black pepper.

NUTRITION PER SERVING

Calories: 390
Carbohydrates: 35g
Sugars: 6g
Dietary fiber: 8g
Protein: 16g
Fat: 20g
Cholesterol: 20mg
Sodium: 1,130mg

This is **traditional** Tex-Mex chili features **masa harina,** a corn flour whose unique flavor comes from being soaked in **culinary lime.**

Texas-Style **Chili Con Carne**

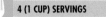

4 (1 CUP) SERVINGS	30 MINUTES	12 MINUTES	2/HIGH

INGREDIENTS

1 TB. olive oil

1 slice smoky bacon, cut into ½-in. (1.25cm) pieces

1½ lb. (680g) flank steak, cut into ½-in. (1.25cm) cubes

1 small yellow onion, diced small (½ cup)

2 TB. minced garlic

3 TB. dark chili powder

1½ tsp. crushed cumin seed

1½ tsp. dried Mexican oregano

4 large roma tomatoes, halved

3 TB. tomato paste

½ tsp. kosher salt

¼ tsp. freshly ground black pepper

½ cup water

¼ cup yellow masa harina, or 1 cup crumbled corn tortillas

1 cup shredded cheddar cheese

1 small red onion, diced small (½ cup)

½ cup sour cream

3 serrano chiles, thinly sliced (¼ cup)

METHOD

1 In a 6-quart (5.5l) pressure cooker set to medium-high (traditional)/ high (electric) heat, add olive oil. Add bacon, and slowly render some fat from bacon, allowing it to become crisp-tender.

2 Add flank steak without crowding it (cook in batches, if necessary), and brown on all sides for 7 minutes.

3 Add yellow onion, stir, and cook for about 3 minutes or for 3 to 5 minutes.

4 Add garlic, dark chili powder, cumin seed, and Mexican oregano, and stir until fragrant.

5 Add roma tomatoes, tomato paste, kosher salt, black pepper, and water, and bring to a boil.

6 Lock on the lid, and bring pressure to level 2 (traditional)/high (electric). Reduce heat to low, and cook at 2/high for 12 minutes.

Remove from (traditional)/turn off (electric) heat, perform a cold water (traditional)/quick (electric) release, and remove the lid.

7 If there's too much liquid, whisk in ¼ cup masa harina; otherwise, use ⅛ cup. Be sure to whisk well to avoid lumps. Taste, add more salt as necessary, and stir. Set heat to medium (traditional)/high (electric), and bring to a boil.

8 Serve with cheddar cheese, red onion, sour cream, and serrano chiles for topping.

NUTRITION PER SERVING

Calories: **590**

Carbohydrates: **20g**

Sugars: **6g**

Dietary fiber: **5g**

Protein: **60g**

Fat: **30g**

Cholesterol: **115mg**

Sodium: **1,080mg**

The **tofu** in this **lively stew** is a nice addition, and you'll be impressed with the amount of **flavor** it absorbs from the **beef broth**.

Korean Beef **Stew**

6 (1 CUP) SERVINGS	30 MINUTES	15 MINUTES	2/HIGH

INGREDIENTS

1 (1½ lb.; 680g) chuck roast, cut into 1-in. (2.5cm) cubes

1½ tsp. kosher salt

2 tsp. dark sesame oil

1 TB. vegetable oil

2 large russet potatoes, cut into ½-in. (1.25cm) pieces

3 medium carrots, peeled and cut into 1-in. (2.5cm) pieces

1 large yellow onion, cut into ½-in. (1.25cm) chunks

1 (1-in; 2.5cm) piece ginger, peeled and minced (1 TB.)

3 TB. minced garlic

1 large Fuji apple, peeled, cored, and grated (½ cup)

½ cup low-sodium soy sauce

2 cups water

½ cup chopped kimchi (optional)

2 serrano chiles, chopped

2 medium green onions, minced (¼ cup)

2 TB. red miso

12 oz. (340g) firm tofu, cut in 1-in. (2.5cm) cubes

Cooked rice noodles, hot

METHOD

1 Season chuck roast all over with 1 teaspoon kosher salt.

2 In a 4-quart (4l) pressure cooker set to medium-high (traditional)/high (electric) heat, heat dark sesame oil and vegetable oil. When hot, add chuck roast, and brown on all sides for 5 minutes.

3 Add russet potatoes, carrots, yellow onion, ginger, and garlic. Stir and sauté for 4 minutes or until garlic and ginger become fragrant.

4 Add Fuji apple, soy sauce, water, and remaining ½ teaspoon kosher salt, and bring to a boil.

5 Lock on the lid, and bring pressure to level 2 (traditional)/high (electric). Reduce heat to low, and cook at 2/high for 15 minutes. Remove from (traditional)/turn off (electric) heat, perform a cold water (traditional)/quick (electric) release, and remove the lid.

6 In a medium bowl, combine kimchi (if using), serrano chiles, and green onions.

7 Remove ½ cup broth from the cooker, add red miso, and stir until dissolved. Pour miso broth back into the cooker, and stir.

8 Add tofu, set heat to low, and warm for 4 minutes.

9 Serve stew over rice noodles, topped with a healthy dollop of kimchi relish.

NUTRITION PER SERVING

Calories: **420**

Carbohydrates: **25g**

Sugars: **4g**

Dietary fiber: **3g**

Protein: **31g**

Fat: **21g**

Cholesterol: **70mg**

Sodium: **1,280mg**

This **simple** but **sensational** vegetable beef soup is full of **fresh vegetables** and **tender beef.** It comes together and cooks quickly.

Vegetable Beef **Soup**

🍴 6 (1½ CUP) SERVINGS	🥄 30 MINUTES	🔥 12 MINUTES	⏲ 2/HIGH

INGREDIENTS

2 tsp. vegetable oil

1 (12 oz.; 340g) beef chuck, cut into ½-in. (1.25cm) cubes

1 medium yellow onion, diced medium (1 cup)

3 medium stalks celery, diced medium (¾ cup)

1 TB. minced garlic

3 medium carrots, peeled and cut into thin rounds (1 cup)

2 russet potatoes, skin on, scrubbed, and cut into ½-in. (1.25cm) cubes

1 (14.5-oz.; 410g) can crushed tomatoes, with juice

1 bay leaf

3 cups homemade or sodium-free beef broth

1 jalapeño chile (optional)

¾ tsp. kosher salt

¼ tsp. freshly ground black pepper

½ cup frozen corn kernels

½ cup frozen peas

METHOD

1 In a 6-quart (5.5l) pressure cooker set to medium-high (traditional)/high (electric) heat, heat vegetable oil. Add beef chuck, and brown on all sides for 5 minutes.

2 Add yellow onion, celery, garlic, carrots, and russet potatoes, and stir. When vegetables are fragrant, add tomatoes with juice, bay leaf, beef broth, and jalapeño (if using). Season with kosher salt and black pepper, and bring to a boil.

3 Lock on the lid, bring pressure to level 2 (traditional)/high (electric), and cook for 12 minutes. Remove from (traditional)/turn off (electric) heat, perform a cold water (traditional)/quick (electric) release, and remove the lid.

4 Remove and discard jalapeño and bay leaf.

5 Add corn and peas, set heat to medium-high (traditional)/high (electric), and warm for 5 minutes. Serve hot.

NUTRITION PER SERVING

Calories: 270

Carbohydrates: 28g

Sugars: 7g

Dietary fiber: 5g

Protein: 17g

Fat: 10g

Cholesterol: 35mg

Sodium: 520mg

Served alongside a **nice Irish soda bread** to soak up all the broth, this **hearty** stew is **simple** yet **satisfying**.

Irish **Stew**

4 (1 CUP) SERVINGS | **20 MINUTES** | **12 MINUTES** | **2/HIGH**

INGREDIENTS

1 (2 lb.; 1kg) boneless leg of lamb, trimmed of sinew and excess fat and cut into 1-in. (2.5cm) cubes

1½ tsp. kosher salt

2 TB. unsalted butter

5 medium carrots, peeled and cut into 1-in. (2.5cm) chunks (2 cups)

1 medium yellow onion, diced large (1 cup)

5 medium Yukon Gold potatoes, halved (2 cups)

¼ freshly ground black pepper

2 tsp. fresh thyme

¾ cup water

METHOD

1 In a large bowl, season lamb with 1 teaspoon kosher salt, and set aside for 20 minutes.

2 In a 4-quart (4l) pressure cooker set to medium-high (traditional)/high (electric) heat, melt unsalted butter until it's sizzling and bubbling. Add ½ of lamb, and brown cubes on all sides for 8 minutes. Transfer browned lamb to a plate, and brown remaining lamb, and transfer remaining browned lamb to the plate.

3 Add carrots, yellow onion, and Yukon Gold potatoes to the cooker, and season with remaining ½ teaspoon kosher salt. Return browned lamb to the pressure cooker, season with black pepper and 1 teaspoon thyme, and stir. Add water, and bring to a boil.

4 Lock on the lid, and bring pressure to level 2 (traditional)/high (electric). Reduce heat to low, and cook at 2/high for 12 minutes. Remove from (traditional)/turn off (electric) heat, perform a cold water (traditional)/quick (electric) release, and remove the lid.

5 Stir gently (potatoes will be very tender), divide into 4 bowls, and sprinkle remaining 1 teaspoon thyme over top. Serve with lots of crusty bread for dipping.

NUTRITION PER SERVING

Calories: 590	Sugars: 8g	Protein: 49g	Cholesterol: 150mg
Carbohydrates: 57g	Dietary fiber: 8g	Fat: 18g	Sodium: 910mg

Ramen dishes are made of many **separately cooked** ingredients. With your pressure cooker, you can serve **hot, tasty ramen,** even on busy weeknights.

Pork **Ramen**

4 (2 CUP) SERVINGS | 45 MINUTES + CURE TIME | 15 MINUTES | 2/HIGH

INGREDIENTS

2 lb. (1kg) boneless country-style pork ribs

1½ tsp. kosher salt

1½ tsp. brown sugar

1 TB. vegetable oil

1 slice smoky bacon

1 cup water

1 (12-oz.; 340g) can low-sodium spice ham, cut into ¼-in. slices

4 cups homemade or sodium-free pork or chicken stock

¼ cup low-sodium soy sauce

12 oz. (340g) Chinese noodles, chuka soba, or spaghetti, cooked and rinsed under cold water

4 large soft-boiled eggs

2 medium carrots, peeled and shredded (1 cup)

1 medium zucchini, shredded (1 cup)

1 Fresno or serrano chile, thinly sliced

3 medium green onions, thinly sliced

METHOD

1 Place pork ribs on a rimmed plate, season on all sides with kosher salt and brown sugar, and refrigerate for at least 2 hours or overnight to cure.

2 In a 4-quart (4l) pressure cooker set to medium-high (traditional)/high (electric) heat, heat vegetable oil. When hot, add pork ribs and brown for 5 minutes on all sides (the deeper brown, the better), being careful not to let sugar burn.

3 Add bacon and water, and bring to a boil.

4 Lock on the lid, bring pressure to level 2 (traditional)/high (electric), and cook for 15 minutes. Remove from (traditional)/turn off (electric) heat, and let pork rest for 15 minutes. Remove the lid.

5 Discard bacon. Transfer pork ribs to a cutting board, and shred using 2 forks.

6 In a medium sauté pan over high heat, fry ham for 5 minutes or until crispy. Remove from heat, and keep warm.

7 Add pork stock and soy sauce to the cooker, set heat to medium-high (traditional)/high (electric), and bring to a boil. Reduce heat to low, and keep very warm.

8 To serve, divide Chinese noodles among 4 bowls. Evenly divide soft-boiled eggs, ham, carrots, zucchini, pork, Fresno chile, and green onions over top.

9 Bring stock back to a very hard boil, ladle over soup, and serve.

NUTRITION PER SERVING

Calories: 1,020
Carbohydrates: 71g
Sugars: 8g
Dietary fiber: 3g
Protein: 75g
Fat: 47g
Cholesterol: 440mg
Sodium: 2,730mg

This **homey** soup is made **comforting** with the addition of **simple herbs,** a bit of **rice,** and **half-and-half.** It's a great choice for cool-weather meals.

Hearty Turkey and Vegetable **Soup**

6 (1½ CUP) SERVINGS	20 MINUTES	8 MINUTES	2/HIGH

INGREDIENTS

2 tsp. vegetable oil

12 oz. (340g) turkey breast, cut into ½-in. (1.25cm) cubes

1 medium yellow onion, diced medium (1 cup)

3 medium stalks celery, diced medium (¾ cup)

1 TB. minced garlic

3 medium carrots, peeled and cut into thin rounds (1 cup)

2 medium russet potatoes, skin on, scrubbed, and cut into ½-in. (1.25cm) cubes

¼ cup long-grain rice

1 bay leaf

½ tsp. dried thyme

4 cups homemade or sodium-free chicken or turkey broth

¾ tsp. kosher salt

¼ tsp. freshly ground black pepper

¼ cup half-and-half

METHOD

1 In a 6-quart (5.5l) pressure cooker set to medium-high (traditional)/high (electric) heat, heat vegetable oil. Add turkey, and brown on all sides for 5 minutes.

2 Add yellow onion, celery, garlic, carrots, and russet potatoes, and stir. When vegetables become fragrant, add long-grain rice, bay leaf, thyme, and chicken broth. Season with kosher salt and black pepper, and bring to a boil.

3 Lock on the lid, bring pressure to level 2 (traditional)/high (electric), and cook for 8 minutes. Remove from (traditional)/turn off (electric) heat, perform a cold water (traditional)/quick (electric) release, and remove the lid.

4 Remove and discard bay leaf.

5 Add half-and-half, stir, set heat to medium (traditional)/high (electric), and cook for 8 minutes. Serve hot.

NUTRITION PER SERVING

Calories: 190

Carbohydrates: 22g

Sugars: 2g

Dietary fiber: 2g

Protein: 18g

Fat: 3.5g

Cholesterol: 40mg

Sodium: 690mg

Fish chowder is a bit **mellower** than traditional clam chowder, but it's equally delicious. And in your pressure cooker, it cooks **in minutes.**

New England **Fish Chowder**

🍴 6 (1¼ CUP) SERVINGS	🥄 30 MINUTES	🔥 7 MINUTES	⏲ 1/LOW

INGREDIENTS

2 thick slices smoky bacon, cut into ½-in. (1.25cm) pieces

2 TB. unsalted butter

1 large yellow onion, diced medium (1 cup)

2 large stalks celery, diced medium (1 cup)

2 tsp. minced garlic

4 medium Yukon Gold potatoes, peeled and diced medium (1½ cups)

½ tsp. kosher salt

¼ tsp. freshly ground black pepper

¼ tsp. fennel seed, crushed

1 bay leaf

½ tsp. dried thyme

12 oz. (340g) cod, tilapia, halibut, or other whitefish, cut into ½-in. (1.25cm) pieces

2 cups clam juice

2 cups water

1 TB. fresh flat-leaf parsley, minced

1 TB. fresh chives, minced

METHOD

1 In a 4-quart (4l) pressure cooker set to medium-high (traditional)/high (electric) heat, add bacon and slowly render fat, allowing bacon to become crisp without burning grease. Pour off all but 1 tablespoon grease.

2 Add unsalted butter, and melt. Add yellow onion, celery, and garlic, and cook for about 3 minutes or until vegetables begin to wilt.

3 Add Yukon Gold potatoes, season with kosher salt and black pepper, and stir until garlic is fragrant.

4 Add fennel seed, bay leaf, thyme, cod, clam juice, and water, and bring to a boil.

5 Lock on the lid, and bring pressure to level 1 (traditional)/low (electric). Reduce heat to low, and cook at 1/low for 7 minutes. Remove from (traditional)/turn off (electric) heat, perform a cold water (traditional)/quick (electric) release, and remove the lid.

6 Divide soup among bowls, top with flat-leaf parsley and chives, and serve.

NUTRITION PER SERVING

Calories: **310**
Carbohydrates: **28g**
Sugars: **3g**
Dietary fiber: **3g**
Protein: **19g**
Fat: **13g**
Cholesterol: **65mg**
Sodium: **330mg**

vegetables

Carrots, green beans, potatoes, cruciferous vegetables, and greens all cook well under pressure. Enjoy the variety of European favorites in this section as well as some uniquely American fare.

Stewed gently, the **fresh vegetables** in this perfect summer side dish release their juices to make a **sublime broth.**

Ratatouille

4 (1 CUP) SERVINGS	30 MINUTES	4 MINUTES	1/LOW

INGREDIENTS

1 medium eggplant, peeled and cut into 1-in. (2.5cm) chunks (2 cups)

¾ tsp. kosher salt

2 TB. olive oil

1 large red onion, cut into wedges (1 cup)

2 medium zucchini, cut into ¾-in. (2cm) rounds (2 cups)

1 medium yellow squash, cut into ¾-in. (2cm) chunks (1 cup)

1 medium red bell pepper, roasted, peeled, ribs and seeds removed, and cut into ½-in. (1.25cm) strips (⅔ cup)

1 TB. minced garlic

6 large plum tomatoes, halved lengthwise and cored (2 cups)

½ cup water

¼ tsp. freshly ground white pepper

¼ cup loosely packed fresh basil leaves, torn

METHOD

1 Place eggplant in a colander, season with ½ teaspoon kosher salt, and toss to distribute salt. Set the colander in the sink, and let eggplant release its bitter water for 20 minutes to 1 hour.

2 In a 6-quart (5.5l) pressure cooker set to medium-high (traditional)/high (electric) heat, heat olive oil. Add eggplant and red onion, stir, and cook for about 3 minutes or until vegetables begin to wilt.

3 Add zucchini, yellow squash, red bell pepper, garlic, plum tomatoes, water, remaining ¼ teaspoon kosher salt, and white pepper. Gently stir, and bring to a boil.

4 Lock on the lid, and bring pressure to level 1 (traditional)/low (electric). Reduce heat to low, and cook at 1/low for 4 minutes. Remove from (traditional)/turn off (electric) heat, perform a cold water (traditional)/quick (electric) release, and remove the lid.

5 Stir in ½ of basil, gently ladle into bowls, top with remaining basil, and serve.

NUTRITION PER SERVING

Calories: **70**

Carbohydrates: **15g**

Sugars: **7g**

Dietary fiber: **6g**

Protein: **3g**

Fat: **0.5g**

Cholesterol: **0mg**

Sodium: **250mg**

Honey, vinegar, and **salt** are all in balance in this **versatile** side dish, making the carrots **sweet** and **flavorful**.

Honey-Glazed **Carrots**

🍴 6 (1⅓ CUP) SERVINGS	🥄 15 MINUTES	🔥 4 MINUTES	⏲ 1/LOW

INGREDIENTS

4 large carrots, peeled and cut into ½-in. (1.25cm) rounds

2 tsp. honey

1 tsp. red wine vinegar

2 TB. unsalted butter

¼ tsp. kosher salt

¼ tsp. freshly ground white pepper

1 tsp. fresh thyme leaves

1 cup water

METHOD

1 In a 4-quart (4l) pressure cooker, combine carrots, honey, red wine vinegar, unsalted butter, kosher salt, white pepper, thyme, and water. Set heat to medium-high (traditional)/high (electric), and bring to a boil.

2 Lock on the lid, and bring pressure to level 1 (traditional)/low (electric). Reduce heat to low, and cook at 1/low for 4 minutes. Remove from (traditional)/turn off (electric) heat, perform a cold water (traditional)/quick (electric) release, and remove the lid.

3 Transfer carrots to a serving bowl, and cover lightly with aluminum foil.

4 Set the pressure cooker to high (traditional)/high (electric) heat, and return to a boil. Cook for about 4 minutes or until liquid is reduced to a syrupy glaze.

5 Spoon hot glaze over carrots, and serve.

NUTRITION PER SERVING

Calories: 60	Sugars: 4g	Protein: 1g	Cholesterol: 10mg
Carbohydrates: 6g	Dietary fiber: 1g	Fat: 4g	Sodium: 115mg

Glazed carrots are a classic **fine dining** dish. The addition of **braised lettuce** gives it a very **European flair.**

Glazed Carrots with
Braised Lettuce

4 (½ CUP) SERVINGS   20 MINUTES   2 MINUTES   2/HIGH

INGREDIENTS

- 10 medium carrots, peeled and cut into 1-in. (2.5cm) barrels (3 cups)
- 1 cup homemade or sodium-free vegetable broth or water, or 1 cup water and ½ sodium-free bouillon cube
- ½ tsp. kosher salt
- 6 to 8 small Bibb lettuce leaves from heart of head
- ½ tsp. honey
- 1 TB. unsalted butter

METHOD

1 In a 4-quart (4l) pressure cooker, combine carrots, vegetable broth, and kosher salt. Set heat to medium-high (traditional)/high (electric), and bring to a boil.

2 Lock on the lid, bring pressure to level 2 (traditional)/high (electric), and cook for 2 minutes. Remove from (traditional)/turn off (electric) heat, perform a cold water (traditional)/quick (electric) release, and remove the lid.

3 Return the cooker to medium (traditional)/high (electric) heat. Add Bibb lettuce leaves, honey, and unsalted butter, and stir until leaves are wilted.

4 Taste, add more salt as needed, and serve.

NUTRITION PER SERVING

Calories: **70**	Sugars: **7g**	Protein: **1g**	Cholesterol: **10mg**
Carbohydrates: **10g**	Dietary fiber: **3g**	Fat: **3g**	Sodium: **390mg**

The **smoky flavor** of the ham (or smoked turkey) infuses the cooking broth in this **country-style** green bean dish.

Southern-Style **Green Beans**

| 4 (1 CUP) SERVINGS | 30 MINUTES | 7 MINUTES | 2/HIGH |

INGREDIENTS

1 TB. vegetable oil

1 medium yellow onion, thinly sliced (1 cup)

1½ cups country ham or smoked turkey thigh, diced large

1 cup water

3 medium russet potatoes, halved and cut into ¾-in. (2cm) half moons (2 cups)

1½ lb. (680g) green beans, trimmed and cut into 1-in. (2.5cm) lengths

½ tsp. kosher salt

¼ tsp. freshly ground black pepper

METHOD

1 In a 6-quart (5.5l) pressure cooker set to medium (traditional)/high (electric) heat, heat vegetable oil. Add yellow onion, and sauté for 5 minutes or until onion begins to soften.

2 Add ham and water, and bring to a boil.

3 Add russet potatoes and green beans, season with kosher salt and black pepper, and return to a boil.

4 Lock on the lid, and bring pressure to level 2 (traditional)/high (electric). Reduce heat to medium-low, and cook at 2/high for 7 minutes. Remove from (traditional)/turn off (electric) heat, perform a cold water (traditional)/quick (electric) release, and remove the lid.

5 Taste, adjust kosher salt or black pepper as needed, and gently mix with a large spoon, being careful not to break potatoes. Serve hot.

NUTRITION PER SERVING

| Calories: 290 | Sugars: 6g | Protein: 18g | Cholesterol: 30mg |
| Carbohydrates: 42g | Dietary fiber: 9g | Fat: 7g | Sodium: 1,520mg |

The simple addition of a **nut crunch topping** transforms these perfectly **tender** green beans to **something elegant.**

Buttered Green Beans
with Nut Crunch Topping

4 (½ CUP) SERVINGS	20 MINUTES	4 MINUTES	1/LOW

INGREDIENTS

3 TB. unsalted butter

½ cup walnuts, hazelnuts, or pecans

½ cup panko breadcrumbs

¾ tsp. kosher salt

¼ tsp. freshly ground black pepper

1 lb. (450g) green beans, trimmed

METHOD

1 In a small sauté pan over medium heat, melt 1½ tablespoons unsalted butter.

2 Add walnuts, panko breadcrumbs, ½ teaspoon kosher salt, and black pepper, and sauté for 2 or 3 minutes or until golden. Transfer mixture to a small bowl.

3 Add a steamer basket to a 4-quart (4l) pressure cooker, fill with the minimum amount of water allowed for your cooker, and add green beans to the basket. Set heat to medium-high (traditional)/high (electric), and bring to a boil.

4 Lock on the lid, bring pressure to level 1 (traditional)/low (electric), and cook for 4 minutes. Remove from (traditional)/turn off (electric) heat, perform a cold water (traditional)/ quick (electric) release, and remove the lid.

5 In a small microwave-safe dish, melt remaining 1½ tablespoons butter in the microwave on high for 20 seconds.

6 Transfer green beans to a bowl, toss with melted butter and remaining ¼ teaspoon kosher salt, sprinkle with nut crunch topping, and serve.

NUTRITION PER SERVING

Calories: 230	Sugars: 4g	Protein: 5g	Cholesterol: 25mg
Carbohydrates: 17g	Dietary fiber: 4g	Fat: 17g	Sodium: 380mg

Pressure cooking quickly and evenly steams potatoes for a **smooth, buttery mash.** The **caramelized onions** add a nice flavor to the finished dish.

Caramelized Onion
Mashed Potatoes

6 (⅔ CUP) SERVINGS	35 MINUTES	8 MINUTES	2/HIGH

INGREDIENTS

1 TB. plus ¼ cup unsalted butter

1 large yellow onion, very thinly sliced (1¼ cups)

1 tsp. kosher salt

10 medium russet potatoes, peeled and cut into 1-in. (2.5cm) half moons (4 cups)

⅓ cup heavy cream, hot

½ cup whole milk, hot

⅛ tsp. freshly ground white pepper

NUTRITION PER SERVING

Calories: 270
Carbohydrates: 31g
Sugars: 3g
Dietary fiber: 2g
Protein: 5g
Fat: 15g
Cholesterol: 45mg
Sodium: 340mg

METHOD

1 In a medium skillet over medium heat, melt 1 tablespoon unsalted butter.

2 Add yellow onion and ½ teaspoon kosher salt, and stir once to break apart onion layers. Reduce heat to medium-low, and cook for 5 minutes. Stir once, and cook for 10 minutes. Repeat until onions are gooey and brown, and set aside.

3 Add a steamer basket to a 4-quart (4l) pressure cooker, pour in 1 cup water, and set heat to medium-high (traditional)/high (electric). Add russet potatoes to the basket, and bring to a boil.

4 Lock on the lid, and bring pressure to level 2 (traditional)/high (electric). Reduce heat to low, and cook at 2/high for 8 minutes. Remove from (traditional)/turn off (electric) heat, perform a cold water (traditional)/quick (electric) release, and remove the lid.

5 Test potatoes for doneness by inserting a knife into a large piece. It should easily pierce potato. If potatoes aren't done, lock on the lid and cook for 2 more minutes. Transfer potatoes to a large bowl, and let them steam dry for 30 seconds.

6 Using a potato masher or an electric mixer on low, mash potatoes.

7 Add remaining ¼ cup unsalted butter, and stir gently while it melts. Add caramelized onions, hot heavy cream, hot whole milk, remaining ½ teaspoon kosher salt, and white pepper, and stir. If potatoes are too thick, add more milk a little at a time and stir between additions until you reach your desired consistency. Serve hot.

The **butter, syrup,** and **vanilla extract** complement the **sweet potatoes** in this **light and lovely** dish.

Mashed Maple **Sweet Potatoes**

🍴 6 (½ CUP) SERVINGS	🥄 15 MINUTES	🔥 5 MINUTES	🕐 2/HIGH

INGREDIENTS

3 large sweet potatoes, peeled and cut into ½-in. (1.25cm) rounds (2½ cups)

3 TB. unsalted butter

3 TB. pure maple syrup

1 tsp. vanilla extract

½ tsp. kosher salt

METHOD

1 Add a steamer basket to a 6-quart (5.5l) pressure cooker, and fill with the minimum amount of water allowed for your cooker. Set heat to medium-high (traditional)/high (electric), and bring to a boil.

2 Add sweet potatoes to the steamer basket, and return to a boil.

3 Lock on the lid, bring pressure to level 2 (traditional)/high (electric), and cook for 5 minutes. Remove from (traditional)/turn off (electric) heat, perform a cold water (traditional)/quick (electric) release, remove the lid, and let sweet potatoes sit for 1 minute to steam dry.

4 Transfer sweet potatoes to a large bowl, and using an electric mixer on medium, blend potatoes for a few seconds.

5 Add unsalted butter, and blend until combined. Stir in maple syrup, vanilla extract, and kosher salt, and serve hot.

NUTRITION PER SERVING

Calories: 110	Sugars: 8g	Protein: 1g	Cholesterol: 15mg
Carbohydrates: 14g	Dietary fiber: 1g	Fat: 6g	Sodium: 180mg

Brussels sprouts are a **nutritious vegetable,** and they're delicious paired with **prosciutto** and **almonds.**

Brussels Sprouts with Almonds and Prosciutto

6 (½ CUP) SERVINGS	30 MINUTES	4 MINUTES	1/LOW

INGREDIENTS

- 4 tsp. unsalted butter
- 1 oz. (25g) prosciutto, minced
- 1 lb. (450g) medium brussels sprouts, stalk ends trimmed and halved lengthwise
- ¼ tsp. kosher salt
- ½ cup water
- ½ cup almonds, toasted and chopped
- ¼ tsp. freshly ground black pepper

METHOD

1 In a 4-quart (4l) pressure cooker set to medium-high (traditional)/high (electric) heat, melt 3 teaspoons unsalted butter. Add prosciutto, and cook for 2 minutes or until crisp.

2 Add brussels sprouts, and sauté for about 3 minutes or until they begin to brown.

3 Season with kosher salt, add water, and bring to a boil.

4 Lock on the lid, and bring pressure to level 1 (traditional)/low (electric). Reduce heat to low, and cook at 1/low for 3 minutes (add 30 more seconds for large sprouts). Remove from (traditional)/turn off (electric) heat, perform a cold water (traditional)/quick (electric) release, and remove the lid.

5 Drain sprouts, and transfer to a serving bowl. Toss with almonds, black pepper, and remaining 1 teaspoon unsalted butter, and serve.

NUTRITION PER SERVING

Calories: 140
Carbohydrates: 8g
Sugars: 2g
Dietary fiber: 4g
Protein: 5g
Fat: 11g
Cholesterol: 10mg
Sodium: 135mg

Kale makes **great salads** and **one-pot meals,** but it's especially good braised with a little **chicken broth** and a **pinch of cloves** until just tender.

Braised **Kale**

4 (½ CUP) SERVINGS	5 MINUTES	10 MINUTES	2/HIGH

INGREDIENTS

2 TB. vegetable oil

2 bunches curly leaf kale, stems removed and leaves chopped (6 to 8 cups)

1½ cups homemade or sodium-free chicken broth

1 pinch ground cloves

½ tsp. kosher salt

METHOD

1 In a 4-quart (4l) pressure cooker set to medium-high (traditional)/high (electric) heat, heat vegetable oil.

2 Add kale, and turn leaves over on themselves to coat with oil.

3 Add chicken broth, cloves, and kosher salt, and turn kale again to distribute seasonings. Bring to a boil.

4 Lock on the lid, bring pressure to level 2 (traditional)/high (electric), and cook for 10 minutes. Remove from (traditional)/turn off (electric) heat, perform a cold water (traditional)/quick (electric) release, and remove the lid.

5 Taste, season with more salt as necessary, stir, and serve.

NUTRITION PER SERVING

Calories: 120	Sugars: 0g	Protein: 5g	Cholesterol: 10mg
Carbohydrates: 10g	Dietary fiber: 2g	Fat: 8g	Sodium: 330mg

The **sweetness** of the **apples** alongside the **braised red cabbage** marries well with **pork** of all kinds (especially pork loin braised in Belgian beer).

Alsatian-Style Braised
Red Cabbage

4 (1 CUP) SERVINGS	30 MINUTES	15 MINUTES	2/HIGH

INGREDIENTS

2 TB. unsalted butter or bacon grease

1 large yellow onion, minced (1 cup)

1 TB. sugar

1 medium head red cabbage, chopped (6 cups)

2 medium green apples, peeled, cored, and diced small (1 cup)

1 large russet potato, peeled and grated (¾ cup)

¾ cup water

2 TB. red wine vinegar

2 TB. red or black currant jam

METHOD

1 In a 6-quart (5.5l) pressure cooker set to medium (traditional)/high (electric) heat, melt unsalted butter.

2 Add yellow onion and sugar, stir, and cook for 6 minutes or until onions begin to brown and sugar begins to caramelize.

3 Add red cabbage, green apples, and russet potato, and stir. Add water, red wine vinegar, and red currant jam, and stir again.

4 Lock on the lid, and bring pressure to level 2 (traditional)/high (electric). Reduce heat to low, and cook at 2/high for 15 minutes. Remove from (traditional)/turn off (electric) heat, perform a cold water (traditional)/quick (electric) release, and remove the lid.

5 Stir, taste, adjust seasoning or add a touch more red wine vinegar if desired, and serve.

NUTRITION PER SERVING

Calories: 290	Sugars: 30g	Protein: 6g	Cholesterol: 15mg	
Carbohydrates: 59g	Dietary fiber: 9g	Fat: 6g	Sodium: 110mg	

This **hearty** side dish goes well with **sausages, pork chops,** and **roasted meats.** It's also good as a **light dinner** served on its own.

One-Pot Cabbage,
Rice, and Lentils

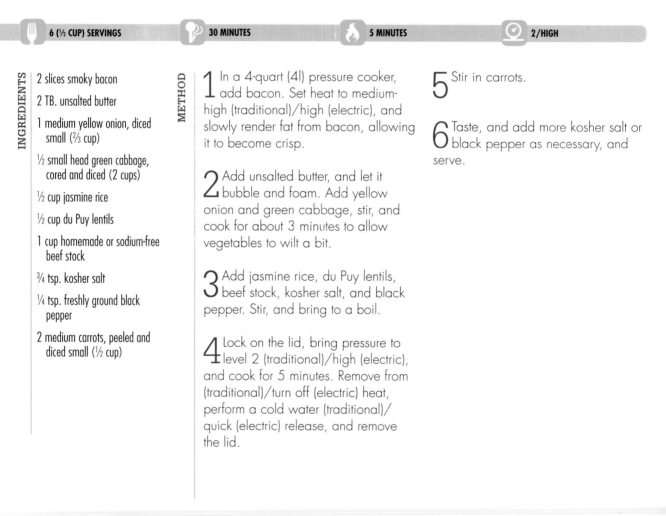

6 (½ CUP) SERVINGS — **30 MINUTES** — **5 MINUTES** — **2/HIGH**

INGREDIENTS

2 slices smoky bacon

2 TB. unsalted butter

1 medium yellow onion, diced small (⅔ cup)

½ small head green cabbage, cored and diced (2 cups)

½ cup jasmine rice

½ cup du Puy lentils

1 cup homemade or sodium-free beef stock

¾ tsp. kosher salt

¼ tsp. freshly ground black pepper

2 medium carrots, peeled and diced small (½ cup)

METHOD

1 In a 4-quart (4l) pressure cooker, add bacon. Set heat to medium-high (traditional)/high (electric), and slowly render fat from bacon, allowing it to become crisp.

2 Add unsalted butter, and let it bubble and foam. Add yellow onion and green cabbage, stir, and cook for about 3 minutes to allow vegetables to wilt a bit.

3 Add jasmine rice, du Puy lentils, beef stock, kosher salt, and black pepper. Stir, and bring to a boil.

4 Lock on the lid, bring pressure to level 2 (traditional)/high (electric), and cook for 5 minutes. Remove from (traditional)/turn off (electric) heat, perform a cold water (traditional)/ quick (electric) release, and remove the lid.

5 Stir in carrots.

6 Taste, and add more kosher salt or black pepper as necessary, and serve.

NUTRITION PER SERVING

Calories: 220	Sugars: 6g	Protein: 8g	Cholesterol: 15mg
Carbohydrates: 31g	Dietary fiber: 6g	Fat: 8g	Sodium: 360mg

Few dishes are more **satisfying** than **collard greens.** In your pressure cooker, collards become **tender** and **meaty.**

Southern **Collard Greens**

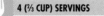

4 (⅔ CUP) SERVINGS	15 MINUTES	42 MINUTES	2/HIGH

INGREDIENTS

2 cups water

1 (8-oz.; 225g) smoked ham hock

½ tsp. kosher salt

¼ tsp. freshly ground black pepper

1 tsp. crushed red pepper flakes

2 small bunches collard greens, stems removed and chopped (8 cups)

METHOD

1 In a 6-quart (5.5l) pressure cooker, combine water and ham hock. Set heat to medium (traditional)/high (electric), and bring to a boil.

2 Lock on the lid, bring pressure to level 2 (traditional)/high (electric), and cook for 30 minutes. Remove from (traditional)/turn off (electric) heat, perform a cold water (traditional)/quick (electric) release, and remove the lid.

3 Add kosher salt, black pepper, crushed red pepper flakes, and collard greens. Using tongs, turn collards to coat with broth.

4 Lock on the lid, return pressure to level 2/high, and cook for 12 minutes. Remove from heat, perform a quick release, and remove the lid.

5 Transfer ham hock to a cutting board. Place the lid loosely back on the pressure cooker.

6 Slice off pork skin, pull meat from the bone, and chop meat finely. Return meat to the pressure cooker, and stir.

7 Taste, adjust seasoning as necessary, and serve.

NUTRITION PER SERVING

Calories: 150	Sugars: 0g	Protein: 5g	Cholesterol: 20mg
Carbohydrates: 4g	Dietary fiber: 3g	Fat: 13g	Sodium: 500mg

meaty main
dishes

Comforting beef and chicken dinners, light and healthy fish dishes, and flavorful entrées from all over the world are easily adaptable to pressure cooking. In fact, your pressure cooker excels at cooking meats quickly while sealing in natural juices.

These **short ribs** are a perfect match for your pressure cooker. They come out **juicy, tender,** and **succulent** in under an hour.

Barbecue Braised **Short Ribs**

🍴 6 (1 RIB + SAUCE) SERVINGS	🍳 5 MINUTES	🔥 40 MINUTES	⏲ 2/HIGH

INGREDIENTS

3 lb. (1.5kg) beef short ribs

2 tsp. kosher salt

1 TB. vegetable oil

1 large yellow onion, thinly sliced (1 cup)

1 cup water

½ cup barbecue sauce

METHOD

1 Season beef short ribs on all sides with 1½ teaspoons kosher salt, and set aside until salt is absorbed.

2 In a 6-quart (5.5l) pressure cooker set to medium-high (traditional)/ high (electric) heat, heat vegetable oil. When hot and nearly smoking, add ribs, leaving space between them so they brown nicely and don't steam. (You might need to do this in batches.) Transfer browned ribs to a baking sheet, and set aside.

3 Add yellow onion to the cooker, and cook for about 3 minutes or until it begins to wilt.

4 Season onion with remaining ½ teaspoon kosher salt, and add ribs and water.

5 Lock on the lid, and bring pressure to level 2 (traditional)/high (electric). Reduce heat to low, and cook at 2/high for 40 minutes. Remove from (traditional)/turn off (electric) heat, perform a quick release, and remove the lid.

6 Gently transfer ribs to a large plate, and drain off all but 3 tablespoons liquid from onions.

7 Add barbecue sauce to onions, and stir. Return ribs to the pressure cooker, turn ribs to coat in sauce, and heat for about 5 minutes. Serve hot.

NUTRITION PER SERVING

Calories: **470**	Sugars: **1g**	Protein: **48g**	Cholesterol: **150mg**
Carbohydrates: **4g**	Dietary fiber: **0g**	Fat: **28g**	Sodium: **1,030mg**

Basil, oregano, rosemary, spices, and **yellow onion** flavor a simple yet rich and satisfying sauce that's served over **spaghetti**.

Beef **Sugo**

6 (½ CUP) SERVINGS | **15 MINUTES** | **45 MINUTES** | **2/HIGH**

INGREDIENTS

1 (3-lb.; 2.5kg) chuck roast

2 tsp. kosher salt

1 TB. unsalted butter

1 medium yellow onion, cut into thick wedges

3½ cups strained tomatoes

2 tsp. dried rosemary, coarsely ground

1½ tsp. dried oregano

1 tsp. dried basil

¼ tsp. freshly ground black pepper

1 lb. (450g) cooked spaghetti, hot

½ cup grated Parmesan cheese

METHOD

1 Season chuck roast on both sides with 1 teaspoon kosher salt, and set aside until salt is absorbed.

2 In a 6-quart (5.5l) pressure cooker set to medium-high (traditional)/ high (electric) heat, heat unsalted butter until it starts to bubble. Add chuck roast, and brown on both sides for about 4 minutes.

3 Add yellow onion, and cook for 3 to 5 minutes or until it wilts.

4 Add strained tomatoes, rosemary, oregano, basil, remaining 1 teaspoon kosher salt, and black pepper, and bring to a boil.

5 Lock on the lid, and bring pressure to level 2 (traditional)/high (electric). Reduce heat to low, and cook at 2/high for 45 minutes. Remove from (traditional)/turn off (electric) heat, perform a natural release, and remove the lid.

6 Transfer beef to a baking sheet, and shred using 2 forks. Return shredded beef to sauce, and stir.

7 Divide spaghetti among 6 plates, top with sauce, and serve with Parmesan cheese on the side.

NUTRITION PER SERVING

Calories: **780**

Carbohydrates: **57g**

Sugars: **4g**

Dietary fiber: **2g**

Protein: **57g**

Fat: **34g**

Cholesterol: **125mg**

Sodium: **820mg**

This **New England boiled dinner,** with corned beef, cabbage, and vegetables, makes a very **filling meal.**

Corned **Beef**

| 4 (3 SLICE + VEGETABLE) SERVINGS | 30 MINUTES | 47 MINUTES | 2/HIGH |

INGREDIENTS

1 (3-lb.; 1.5kg) corned beef brisket

2 cups water

1 TB. pickling spice

2 medium yellow onions, quartered (2 cups)

8 medium Yukon Gold potatoes, halved

8 medium carrots, peeled and cut into 2-in. (5cm) pieces (2½ cups)

1 small head green cabbage, quartered

Kosher salt

Dijon mustard

Unsalted butter

METHOD

1 In a 6-quart (5.5l) pressure cooker, combine corned beef brisket, water, pickling spice, and 2 yellow onion quarters. Set heat to medium-high (traditional)/high (electric), and bring to a boil.

2 Lock on the lid, and bring pressure to level 2 (traditional)/high (electric). Reduce heat to low, and cook at 2/high for 35 minutes. Remove from (traditional)/turn off (electric) heat, perform a cold water (traditional)/quick (electric) release, and remove the lid.

3 Add remaining yellow onion quarters, Yukon Gold potatoes, carrots, and green cabbage, in that order, and season with kosher salt. Return the pressure cooker to medium-high/high heat, and bring to a boil.

4 Lock on the lid, and bring pressure to level 2/high. Reduce heat to low, and cook at 2/high for 12 minutes. Remove from/turn off heat, perform a cold water/quick release, and remove the lid.

5 Transfer corned beef to a cutting board, slice thinly, and place on a platter. Surround meat with vegetables, and ladle some juice from the cooker over top. Serve with Dijon mustard, unsalted butter, and kosher salt on the side.

To prepare the corned beef brisket without additional vegetables, cook it straight through for 45 minutes.

NUTRITION PER SERVING

| Calories: **1,110** | Sugars: **14g** | Protein: **62g** | Cholesterol: **185mg** |
| Carbohydrates: **100g** | Dietary fiber: **12g** | Fat: **51g** | Sodium: **4,260mg** |

Ropa vieja encompasses all the flavors associated with **Cuban cuisine** and is commonly served with **rice and peas, bread,** and **red wine.**

Cuban-Style **Ropa Vieja**

4 (1½ CUP) SERVINGS | **30 MINUTES** | **45 MINUTES** | **2/HIGH**

INGREDIENTS

1 (1½-lb.; 680g) top round steak, well marbled

½ tsp. kosher salt

3 TB. olive oil

2 small yellow onions, diced small (1 cup)

1 medium carrot, peeled and diced small (⅓ cup)

1 bay leaf

½ tsp. crushed cumin

1 (6-oz.; 170g) can tomato paste

1 tsp. dried oregano

½ tsp. dried thyme

1 TB. minced garlic

¾ cup homemade or sodium-free beef stock, or water

½ cup green olives, pitted and halved

1 Fresno or jalapeño chile, chopped

1 TB. capers, rinsed and coarsely chopped

2 TB. fresh cilantro, minced

1 TB. red wine vinegar

1 small red onion, diced fine (¼ cup)

1 large lime, quartered

METHOD

1 Season top round steak with kosher salt, and set aside until salt is absorbed.

2 In a 6-quart (5.5l) pressure cooker set to medium-high (traditional)/ high (electric) heat, heat 1 tablespoon olive oil. When hot, add top round steak, and sear on both sides for 4 minutes or until very brown.

3 Add yellow onions and carrot, and cook for about 3 minutes or until vegetables begin to soften.

4 Add bay leaf, cumin, tomato paste, oregano, thyme, and garlic, and stir until fragrant. Add beef stock, and bring to a boil.

5 Lock on the lid, and bring pressure to level 2 (traditional)/high (electric). Reduce heat to low, and cook at 2/high for 45 minutes. Remove from (traditional)/turn off (electric) heat, perform a cold water (traditional)/quick (electric) release, and remove the lid.

6 In a small bowl, combine green olives, Fresno chile, capers, cilantro, red wine vinegar, red onion, and remaining 2 tablespoons olive oil. Set aside for 10 minutes.

7 Transfer beef to a cutting board, and shred using 2 forks. Return beef to the cooker, and stir to coat in broth. Remove bay leaf.

8 Garnish with green olive salsa, and serve hot with lime quarters on the side.

Traditionally, ropa vieja uses flank steak, but less-expensive top round steak works well in your pressure cooker.

NUTRITION PER SERVING

Calories: **460**

Carbohydrates: **17g**

Sugars: **9g**

Dietary fiber: **3g**

Protein: **42g**

Fat: **25g**

Cholesterol: **85mg**

Sodium: **870mg**

For a **tender, juicy brisket** you'll be proud to serve at family or holiday dinners, opt for a **second cut,** which contains more pressure cooker–friendly fat.

Classic **Beef Brisket**

🍴 6 (3 OR 4 SLICE) SERVINGS	🥄 15 MINUTES	🔥 40 TO 50 MINUTES	⏲ 2/HIGH

INGREDIENTS

1 (3½-lb.; 1.75kg) beef brisket

2½ tsp. kosher salt

1½ TB. canola oil

2 large yellow onions, sliced (3 cups)

½ tsp. dried thyme

¼ tsp. freshly ground black pepper

1½ cups water

METHOD

1 Season beef brisket with 2 teaspoons kosher salt, and set aside until salt is absorbed.

2 Set a 4-quart (4l) pressure cooker to medium-high (traditional)/high (electric) heat. When hot, add canola oil. Carefully add brisket, fat side down, and sear for 4 minutes or until fat is very brown. (Reduce heat if necessary to avoid burning oil.) Turn over brisket, and brown meat side for 4 minutes. Transfer browned brisket to a tray.

3 Drain off most of oil from the pressure cooker.

4 Set heat to medium-low (traditional)/low (electric), and add yellow onions. Season with thyme, remaining ½ teaspoon kosher salt, and black pepper, and cook for 10 minutes or until onions begin to brown and become soft.

5 Place brisket on top of onions, add water, and bring to a boil.

6 Lock on the lid, and bring pressure to level 2 (traditional)/high (electric). Reduce heat to low, and cook at 2/high for 40 minutes for sliced brisket or 50 minutes for shredded beef. Remove from (traditional)/turn off (electric) heat, perform a cold water (traditional)/quick (electric) release, and remove the lid.

7 Transfer brisket to a platter, slice or shred, and serve hot.

NUTRITION PER SERVING

Calories: 320	Sugars: 3g	Protein: 50g	Cholesterol: 100mg
Carbohydrates: 7g	Dietary fiber: 1g	Fat: 9g	Sodium: 970mg

Beef and fennel are naturals together. This **pot roast** is perfect for chilly evenings when you want to **warm your family** from the inside out.

Pot Roast with Fennel and Carrots

4 (3 SLICE + VEGETABLE) SERVINGS	30 MINUTES	45 MINUTES	2/HIGH

INGREDIENTS

1 (3½-lb.; 1.75kg) boneless chuck roast

1 tsp. kosher salt

1 TB. olive oil

1 medium bulb fennel, cored and diced small (¾ cup)

1 large yellow onion, diced small (1 cup)

1 tsp. dried rosemary

1½ tsp. crushed fennel seed

1 TB. red wine vinegar

1 TB. tomato paste

1 cup homemade or sodium-free beef stock

¼ tsp. freshly ground black pepper

6 medium carrots, peeled and cut into 1-in. (2.5cm) cylinders (2 cups)

Fennel fronds

METHOD

1 Season chuck roast on both sides with ½ teaspoon kosher salt, and set aside until salt is absorbed.

2 In a 6-quart (5.5l) pressure cooker set to medium-high (traditional)/high (electric) heat, heat olive oil. Add chuck roast, and brown very deeply on both sides for 5 minutes.

3 Add fennel and yellow onion, stir, and cook for 4 minutes or until vegetables are soft.

4 Add rosemary, fennel seed, red wine vinegar, and tomato paste, and cook for 30 seconds or until seasonings are fragrant.

5 Add beef stock, remaining ½ teaspoon kosher salt, and black pepper, and bring to a boil.

6 Lock on the lid, and bring pressure to level 2 (traditional)/high (electric). Reduce heat to low, and cook for 30 minutes. Remove from (traditional)/turn off (electric) heat, perform a cold water (traditional)/quick (electric) release, and remove the lid.

7 Add carrots.

8 Lock on the lid, and bring pressure to level 2/high. Reduce heat to low, and cook at 2/high for 15 minutes. Remove from/turn off heat, perform a quick release, and remove the lid.

9 Transfer roast to a cutting board, slice thinly, and place on a platter. Surround with carrots, ladle *jus* over top, garnish with fennel, and serve.

NUTRITION PER SERVING

Calories: 870	Sugars: 6g	Protein: 78g	Cholesterol: 245mg
Carbohydrates: 16g	Dietary fiber: 5g	Fat: 54g	Sodium: 730mg

This Scandinavian fare is often served as an **hors d'oeuvre,** but it's even better for **dinner.** These meatballs are **full of flavor** but not overly spicy.

Swedish **Meatballs**

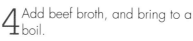

| 4 (3 MEATBALL + SAUCE) SERVINGS | 30 MINUTES | 5 MINUTES | 2/HIGH |

INGREDIENTS

- 1 lb. lean (85% lean) ground chuck
- ¼ lb. lean ground pork
- ⅓ cup unseasoned breadcrumbs
- 2 TB. heavy cream
- 1 tsp. kosher salt
- 1 small yellow onion, diced fine (⅓ cup)
- ¼ tsp. freshly ground black pepper
- ½ tsp. allspice
- ⅛ tsp. nutmeg
- 1 TB. canola oil
- 1 cup homemade or sodium-free beef broth
- ¼ cup sour cream
- 1 TB. fresh dill, minced

METHOD

1. In a large bowl, combine ground chuck, ground pork, unseasoned breadcrumbs, heavy cream, kosher salt, yellow onion, black pepper, allspice, and nutmeg.

2. With clean, wet hands, scoop out a golf ball–size piece of meat mixture, roll it in the palms of your hands until it's a smooth ball, and set aside. Repeat with remaining meat mixture until you have 12 equal-size meatballs.

3. Set a 4-quart (4l) pressure cooker to medium-high (traditional)/high (electric) heat. When hot, add canola oil. Add meatballs, and brown on all sides for 5 minutes. (Reduce heat if necessary to avoid oil smoking.)

4. Add beef broth, and bring to a boil.

5. Lock on the lid, and bring pressure to level 2 (traditional)/high (electric). Reduce heat to low, and cook at 2/high for 5 minutes. Remove from (traditional)/turn off (electric) heat, perform a quick release, and remove the lid.

6. Transfer meatballs to a plate.

7. Whisk sour cream into broth until smooth. Add dill, return meatballs to sauce, and stir to coat and warm. (Do not let sauce come to a boil or it might separate.) Serve hot over rice.

NUTRITION PER SERVING

| Calories: 390 | Sugars: 2g | Protein: 27g | Cholesterol: 110mg |
| Carbohydrates: 9g | Dietary fiber: 1g | Fat: 26g | Sodium: 660mg |

Your pressure cooker makes quick work of this **classic beef, red wine, onion, and mushroom** dish.

Beef **Bourguignon**

🍴 4 (1½ CUP) SERVINGS	🥣 15 MINUTES	🔥 30 MINUTES	⏱ 2/HIGH

INGREDIENTS

1 (2½-lb.; 1.25kg) beef chuck, cut into 2-in. (5cm) cubes

1½ tsp. kosher salt

¼ tsp. freshly ground black pepper

3 TB. unsalted butter

8 oz. (225g) small white mushrooms, brushed clean

24 small pearl onions, peeled

1½ TB. all-purpose flour

1 TB. tomato paste

1 cup dry red wine

1 cup homemade or sodium-free beef stock

15 sprigs thyme

1 bay leaf

METHOD

1 Season beef chuck with 1 teaspoon kosher salt and black pepper, and set aside until salt is absorbed.

2 In a 6-quart (5.5l) pressure cooker set to medium-high (traditional)/ high (electric) heat, melt 2 tablespoons unsalted butter. Add ½ of beef chuck, and brown on all sides for 4 minutes. Transfer browned beef to a plate, repeat with remaining beef, and transfer rest of browned beef to the plate.

3 Add remaining 1 tablespoon unsalted butter, white mushrooms, pearl onions, and remaining ½ teaspoon kosher salt to the cooker, and cook for 5 minutes or until vegetables brown slightly.

4 Add all-purpose flour, and stir to coat vegetables in flour. Add tomato paste, and stir again. Add red wine, bring to a boil, and burn off alcohol for 2 minutes.

5 Add beef stock, browned beef, ½ of thyme sprigs, and bay leaf, and bring to a boil.

6 Lock on the lid, and bring pressure to level 2 (traditional)/high (electric). Reduce heat to low, and cook at 2/high for 30 minutes. Remove from (traditional)/turn off (electric) heat, perform a cold water (traditional)/quick (electric) release, and remove the lid.

7 Remove bay leaf. Divide beef, mushrooms, and onions evenly among 4 bowls, and ladle broth over top. Remove thyme leaves from stems, sprinkle leaves over top of each bowl, and serve.

NUTRITION PER SERVING

Calories: 740	Sugars: 5g	Protein: 56g	Cholesterol: 200mg
Carbohydrates: 15g	Dietary fiber: 0g	Fat: 44g	Sodium: 890mg

An ideal Sunday supper dish, this **eastern European–inspired** recipe combines **tender beef** and **carrots** with **garlic, marjoram,** and **horseradish.**

Chuck Roast with Horseradish Cream and Carrots

4 (4 SLICE + VEGETABLE) SERVINGS	30 MINUTES	19 MINUTES	2/HIGH

INGREDIENTS

1 (2½-lb.; 1.75kg) chuck roast

½ tsp. kosher salt

1 TB. vegetable oil

2 tsp. minced garlic

1 cup homemade or sodium-free beef stock

½ tsp. dried marjoram

2 tsp. prepared horseradish

4 large carrots, peeled and cut into 3-in. (7.5cm) sticks

¼ cup heavy cream (optional)

NUTRITION PER SERVING

Calories: 610
Carbohydrates: 7g
Sugars: 3g
Dietary fiber: 2g
Protein: 55g
Fat: 39g
Cholesterol: 175mg
Sodium: 650mg

METHOD

1 Season chuck roast with kosher salt, and set aside until salt is absorbed.

2 In a 6-quart (5.5l) pressure cooker set to medium-high (traditional)/high (electric) heat, heat vegetable oil. When hot, add chuck roast, and brown deeply for 3 minutes. Turn over roast, and brown other side for 3 minutes.

3 Add garlic, and cook for 10 seconds or until fragrant.

4 Add beef stock, marjoram, and horseradish. Stir, and bring to a boil.

5 Lock on the lid, and bring pressure to level 2 (traditional)/high (electric). Reduce heat to low, and cook at 2/high for 15 minutes. Remove from (traditional)/turn off (electric) heat, perform a cold water (traditional)/quick (electric) release, and remove the lid.

6 Add carrots.

7 Lock on the lid, and return pressure to level 2/high. Reduce heat to low, and cook at 2/high for 4 minutes. Remove from/turn off heat, perform a cold water/quick release, and remove the lid.

8 Transfer roast to a platter, and surround with carrots. Cover with aluminum foil to keep warm, and set aside.

9 Add heavy cream (if using) to the pressure cooker, set heat to high (traditional)/high (electric), and cook for 5 minutes or until sauce is reduced by half. Taste, and add kosher salt as necessary.

10 Slice roast, ladle sauce over top, and serve.

Top sirloin and **vegetables** transform to succulent Swiss steak in your pressure cooker. If you like, add 1 cup sliced **button mushrooms** with the vegetables.

Swiss **Steak**

🍴 4 (4 SLICE + VEGETABLE) SERVINGS	🌀 30 MINUTES	🔥 10 MINUTES	⏱ 2/HIGH

INGREDIENTS

1 (2-lb.; 1kg) top sirloin, 1 in. (2.5cm) thick

1 tsp. kosher salt

1 TB. vegetable oil

2 medium yellow onions, sliced thin (1½ cups)

1 large red bell pepper, ribs and seeds removed, and thinly sliced (¾ cup)

2 medium stalks celery, thinly sliced (½ cup)

3 cloves garlic, minced

¼ tsp. freshly ground black pepper

1 cup homemade or sodium-free beef broth

1 TB. cornstarch

2 TB. cold water

METHOD

1 Season top sirloin on both sides with ½ teaspoon kosher salt, and set aside until salt is absorbed.

2 In a 6-quart (5.5l) pressure cooker set to medium-high (traditional)/ high (electric) heat, heat vegetable oil. When hot, add sirloin, and sear on both sides for 4 minutes or until very brown. Transfer sirloin to a tray.

3 Pour off fat from the pressure cooker. Add yellow onions, red bell pepper, celery, garlic, black pepper, and remaining ½ teaspoon kosher salt. Sauté for about 3 minutes or until vegetables are wilted.

4 Set sirloin on vegetables, add beef broth, and bring to a boil.

5 Lock on the lid, bring pressure to level 2 (traditional)/high (electric), and cook for 10 minutes. Remove from (traditional)/turn off (electric) heat, perform a cold water (traditional)/quick (electric) release, and remove the lid.

6 Transfer sirloin to a cutting board, and cover with aluminum foil to keep warm.

7 In a small bowl, combine cornstarch and cold water.

8 Return the pressure cooker to medium-high/high heat, and bring to a boil. Stir in cornstarch mixture, and return to a boil. Reduce heat to a simmer, and cook for 1 minute to thicken.

9 Slice steak, arrange on a platter, ladle sauce over top, and serve.

NUTRITION PER SERVING

Calories: **500**	Sugars: **4g**	Protein: **68g**	Cholesterol: **185mg**
Carbohydrates: **11g**	Dietary fiber: **2g**	Fat: **21g**	Sodium: **1,300mg**

This Italian braised **veal** and **vegetable** dish is **rich** with **flavorful broth.** It's especially good served with **Risotto Milanese** on the side.

Osso **Buco**

4 (1 SHANK) SERVINGS	30 MINUTES	30 MINUTES	2/HIGH

INGREDIENTS

4 (12-oz.; 340g) meaty veal shanks (osso buco cut)

1½ tsp. kosher salt

1 TB. vegetable oil

1 large yellow onion, diced medium (1½ cups)

2 medium carrots, peeled and cut into rounds (¾ cup)

2 medium stalks celery, cut into thin half-moons (¾ cup)

2 cloves garlic, minced

1½ tsp. dried rosemary, ground

½ tsp. dried sage, ground

2 TB. tomato paste

¾ cup homemade or sodium-free beef broth

¼ tsp. freshly ground black pepper

METHOD

1 Season veal shanks with ¾ teaspoon kosher salt, and set aside until salt is absorbed.

2 In a 6-quart (5.5l) pressure cooker set to medium-high (traditional)/ high (electric) heat, heat vegetable oil. When hot, carefully add shanks, and brown on all sides for 4 minutes. (You might need to do this in batches.) Transfer browned veal to a tray.

3 Add yellow onion, carrots, celery, and garlic to the cooker, and cook for about 4 minutes or until wilted.

4 Add rosemary and sage, and cook for about 30 seconds or until fragrant.

5 Add tomato paste, and stir. Add beef broth, remaining ¾ teaspoon kosher salt, and black pepper, and place veal on top of vegetables. Bring to a boil.

6 Lock on the lid, bring pressure to level 2 (traditional)/high (electric), and cook for 30 minutes. Remove from (traditional)/turn off (electric) heat, perform a cold water (traditional)/quick (electric) release, and remove the lid.

7 Check veal tenderness by inserting a knife; it should pierce meat easily. If necessary, lock on lid, bring to high/2 pressure, and cook for 10 more minutes.

8 Taste broth, and season with salt as necessary. Serve veal with broth over top.

NUTRITION PER SERVING

Calories: 350	Sugars: 5g	Protein: 48g	Cholesterol: 180mg
Carbohydrates: 10g	Dietary fiber: 2g	Fat: 12g	Sodium: 1,140mg

This **traditional** Belgian dish, also known as *carbonnade*, relies on the **deep flavors** of the **Belgian beer** to differentiate it from beef bourguignon.

Belgian Beef Stew
Cooked in Beer

| 4 (1½ CUP) SERVINGS | 15 MINUTES | 35 MINUTES | 2/HIGH |

INGREDIENTS

1 (2½-lb.; 1.25kg) beef chuck, cut into 2-in. (5cm) cubes

1½ tsp. kosher salt

¼ tsp. freshly ground black pepper

3 TB. unsalted butter

2 large yellow onions, sliced (3 cups)

1½ TB. all-purpose flour

1 tsp. brown sugar

1 TB. Dijon mustard

1½ cups Belgian farmhouse ale

1 cup homemade or sodium-free beef stock

1 bay leaf

15 sprigs thyme

METHOD

1 Season beef chuck with 1 teaspoon kosher salt and black pepper, and set aside until salt is absorbed.

2 In a 6-quart (5.5l) pressure cooker set to medium-high (traditional)/ high (electric) heat, melt 2 tablespoons unsalted butter. Add ½ of beef, and brown on all sides for 4 minutes. Transfer browned beef to a plate, repeat with remaining beef, and transfer rest of browned beef to the plate.

3 Add remaining 1 tablespoon unsalted butter, yellow onions, and remaining ½ teaspoon salt to the cooker, and cook for 5 minutes or until onions are slightly brown.

4 Add all-purpose flour, and stir to coat. Stir in brown sugar, Dijon mustard, and Belgian farmhouse ale. Bring to a boil, and burn off alcohol for 1 minute.

5 Add beef stock, beef, bay leaf, and ½ of thyme, and bring to a boil.

6 Lock on the lid, and bring pressure to level 2 (traditional)/high (electric). Reduce heat to low, and cook at 2/high for 30 minutes. Remove from (traditional)/turn off (electric) heat, perform a cold water (traditional)/quick (electric) release, and remove the lid.

7 Remove bay leaf. Divide beef and onions evenly among 4 bowls, and ladle broth over top. Remove thyme leaves from remaining stems, sprinkle leaves over each serving, and serve.

NUTRITION PER SERVING

| Calories: 720 | Sugars: 5g | Protein: 56g | Cholesterol: 200mg |
| Carbohydrates: 14g | Dietary fiber: 1g | Fat: 44g | Sodium: 300mg |

By using **pork ribs** instead of ground beef, this taco meat is much closer to **traditional Mexican fare.** This kid-friendly recipe is very mild, heat-wise.

Pressure Cooker **Tacos**

8 (2 TACO) SERVINGS	30 MINUTES + BRINE TIME	40 MINUTES	2/HIGH

INGREDIENTS

3 (1¼-lb.; 565g) boneless country-style pork shoulder ribs

1 TB. kosher salt

1 TB. ground cumin

1 TB. dried oregano, coarsely ground

1½ TB. mild chili powder

1 TB. vegetable oil

1 cup water

16 (6-in.; 16.25cm) corn or (8-in.; 20cm) flour tortillas

2 medium limes, quartered

Toppings and condiments: sour cream, thinly sliced cabbage, salsa, shredded cheese, thinly sliced radishes, sliced chile peppers

METHOD

1 Season pork shoulder ribs on all sides with kosher salt, and set aside until salt is absorbed.

2 In a small bowl, combine cumin, oregano, and chili powder. Season ribs on all sides with spice mix, and refrigerate for 2 hours or overnight.

3 In a 6-quart (5.5l) pressure cooker set to medium-high (traditional)/ high (electric) heat, heat vegetable oil, swirling the cooker gently to coat. Add ribs, and brown on all sides for 4 minutes. Add water.

4 Lock on the lid, bring pressure to level 2 (traditional)/high (electric), and cook for 40 minutes. Remove from (traditional)/turn off (electric) heat, perform a cold water (traditional)/quick (electric) or natural release, and remove the lid.

5 Wrap corn tortillas in aluminum foil and warm in a 200°F (90°C) oven for 10 minutes.

6 Transfer ribs to a plate, and shred meat into small pieces using 2 forks. Place meat in a bowl, and stir in ½ cup or more juice from the cooker.

7 Serve meat alongside lime quarters and your choice of toppings and condiments, allowing everyone to make their own tacos.

NUTRITION PER SERVING

Calories: 450	Sugars: 0g	Protein: 44g	Cholesterol: 140mg
Carbohydrates: 28g	Dietary fiber: 2g	Fat: 17g	Sodium: 960mg

These elegant stuffed peppers are **incredibly delicious** and very **eastern European** in flavor.

Hungarian **Stuffed Peppers**

8 (½ PEPPER) SERVINGS | 40 MINUTES | 15 MINUTES | 2/HIGH

INGREDIENTS

4 medium red bell peppers

2 slices white bread, torn into small pieces (1 cup)

¼ cup plus 2 TB. heavy cream (2 TB. optional)

1 medium green onion, sliced into thin rings (3 TB.)

¼ cup grated Parmesan cheese

¼ tsp. dried rosemary

⅛ tsp. caraway seed, ground

⅓ cup raisins

2 TB. minced fresh flat-leaf parsley

¾ cup walnuts, chopped

1¼ tsp. kosher salt

⅛ tsp. plus ¼ tsp. freshly ground black pepper

1¼ lb. (565g) lean (10% fat) ground beef

2 cups tomato sauce

1½ TB. unsalted butter

½ cup panko breadcrumbs

METHOD

1 Add a trivet and steamer basket to a 6-quart (5.5l) pressure cooker, and fill with the minimum amount of water allowed for your cooker.

2 Cut around stem of red bell peppers, keeping the knife parallel to outside edge of pepper as you cut. Remove core, seeds, and ribs.

3 In a large bowl, combine white bread, ¼ cup heavy cream, green onion, Parmesan cheese, rosemary, caraway seed, raisins, flat-leaf parsley, ¼ cup walnuts, ¾ teaspoon kosher salt, and ⅛ teaspoon black pepper. Add ground beef, and combine.

4 Evenly divide filling among peppers, and add peppers to the steamer basket. Be sure water does not touch bottom of peppers. Set heat to medium-high (traditional)/high (electric), and bring to a boil.

5 Lock on the lid, bring pressure to level 2 (traditional)/high (electric), reduce heat to low, and cook at 2/high for 15 minutes. Remove from (traditional)/turn off (electric) heat, perform a cold water (traditional)/quick (electric) release, and set aside for 5 minutes. Remove the lid.

6 In a small saucepan over medium heat, warm tomato sauce and remaining 2 tablespoons heavy cream (if using).

7 In a small sauté pan over medium heat, melt unsalted butter. Add remaining ½ cup walnuts, panko breadcrumbs, remaining ½ teaspoon kosher salt, and remaining ¼ teaspoon black pepper, and sauté for 2 or 3 minutes or until golden.

8 Transfer peppers to a plate, spoon tomato sauce over top, sprinkle with nut crunch topping, and serve.

NUTRITION PER SERVING

Calories: 330	Sugars: 9g	Protein: 20g	Cholesterol: 60mg
Carbohydrates: 20g	Dietary fiber: 3g	Fat: 19g	Sodium: 730mg

This **simple, hearty** chicken stew made with sweet, not hot, paprika is **comforting** rather than spicy. Kids will like it as much as adults will.

Hungarian **Chicken Paprika**

4 (3 STRIP + SAUCE) SERVINGS	30 MINUTES	5 MINUTES	2/HIGH

INGREDIENTS

3 (6-oz.; 170g) chicken breasts, cut into 1-in. (2.5cm) lengthwise strips

¾ tsp. kosher salt

1½ TB. vegetable oil

1 medium red bell pepper, ribs and seeds removed, and finely chopped (½ cup)

1 large yellow onion, finely chopped (1 cup)

3 TB. all-purpose flour

⅛ tsp. freshly ground white pepper

2 TB. sweet paprika

3 TB. tomato paste

½ cup homemade or sodium-free chicken broth

½ cup sour cream

2 TB. fresh flat-leaf parsley, minced

METHOD

1 Season chicken breasts with ½ teaspoon kosher salt, and set aside until salt is absorbed.

2 In a 4-quart (4l) pressure cooker set to medium-high (traditional)/high (electric) heat, heat vegetable oil. Add chicken, and brown for 3 minutes. Transfer browned chicken to a tray.

3 Add red bell pepper and yellow onion to the cooker, and cook for about 4 minutes or until soft and just beginning to brown at edges.

4 Add all-purpose flour, remaining ¼ teaspoon kosher salt, white pepper, sweet paprika, and tomato paste, and cook for 1 minute or until flour becomes pasty and tomato paste browns on the bottom of the cooker.

5 Add chicken broth. Using a wooden spoon, scrape up all bits from the bottom of the cooker. Bring to a boil, add chicken, and return to a boil.

6 Lock on the lid, bring pressure to level 2 (traditional)/high (electric), and cook for 5 minutes. Remove from (traditional)/turn off (electric) heat, perform a cold water (traditional)/quick (electric) release, and remove the lid.

7 Add sour cream and ½ of flat-leaf parsley, and stir to blend.

8 Serve hot over rice, garnished with remaining flat-leaf parsley.

NUTRITION PER SERVING

Calories: 210	Sugars: 5g	Protein: 12g	Cholesterol: 50mg
Carbohydrates: 12g	Dietary fiber: 2g	Fat: 11g	Sodium: 590mg

This curry is **simple, slightly spicy,** and **not heavy,** thanks to the **coconut milk.**
Make it spicier by adding more curry powder and a diced habanero.

Caribbean **Chicken Curry**

6 SERVINGS	30 MINUTES	15 MINUTES	2/HIGH

INGREDIENTS

1 TB. peanut or canola oil

8 skinless chicken thigh and leg quarters

3 large yellow onions, halved and thinly sliced (3½ cups)

1 (2-in; 5cm) piece fresh ginger, peeled and minced (1½ TB.)

¼ cup thinly sliced fresh garlic

6 to 8 sprigs thyme

3 TB. curry powder

8 medium Yukon Gold potatoes, halved

3 cups homemade or sodium-free chicken stock

1 tsp. kosher salt

¼ tsp. freshly ground black pepper

1 TB. fresh chives, minced

METHOD

1 In a 6-quart (5.5l) pressure cooker set to medium-high (traditional)/high (electric) heat, heat peanut oil. When hot, add chicken and sauté for 5 minutes or until brown on both sides. Transfer chicken to a rimmed baking sheet.

2 Add yellow onions, ginger, garlic, and ½ of thyme to the cooker, and cook for 3 minutes or until onions soften.

3 Add curry powder, and stir until fragrant.

4 Return chicken to the cooker, and top with Yukon Gold potatoes. Add chicken stock, kosher salt, and black pepper, and bring to a boil.

5 Lock on the lid, bring pressure to level 2 (traditional)/high (electric), and cook for 15 minutes. Remove from (traditional)/turn off (electric) heat, perform a cold water (traditional)/quick (electric) release, and remove the lid.

6 Serve hot, garnished with chives and remaining thyme.

NUTRITION PER SERVING

Calories: 200	Sugars: 5g	Protein: 21g	Cholesterol: 80mg
Carbohydrates: 15g	Dietary fiber: 3g	Fat: 6g	Sodium: 710mg

One-pot recipes produce a satisfying meal in a **single dish,** saving cleanup time. One-pot pressure cooker meals require **less cook time,** too.

One-Pot Chicken and Sausage **Perloo**

| 8 SERVINGS | 15 MINUTES | 10 MINUTES | 2/HIGH |

INGREDIENTS

8 (5-oz.; 140g) chicken thighs, skin removed

2 tsp. kosher salt

1½ TB. vegetable oil

1 cup diced Andouille sausage or ham

1 small yellow onion, diced fine (⅓ cup)

3 medium cloves garlic, chopped (1 TB.)

1½ cups short-grain rice

¾ cup frozen lima beans

¾ cup frozen corn

2½ cups water

1 bay leaf

½ tsp. dried thyme

¼ tsp. freshly ground black pepper

1 large green onion, sliced (¼ cup)

1 TB. fresh flat-leaf parsley, minced

METHOD

1 Season chicken thighs with 1½ teaspoons kosher salt, and set aside until salt is absorbed.

2 In a 6-quart (5.5l) pressure cooker set to medium-high (traditional)/ high (electric) heat, heat vegetable oil, swirling pan to coat. Add chicken, skin side down, and brown for 3 minutes or until dark. Turn over chicken, and brown other side for 3 minutes. Transfer chicken to a tray.

3 Pour off all but 3 tablespoons greese from the cooker. Add Andouille sausage, yellow onion, and garlic. Stir, and sauté vegetables for about 2 minutes or until they begin to soften.

4 Add short-grain rice, lima beans, and corn, and stir. Stir in water, bay leaf, thyme, black pepper, and remaining ½ teaspoon kosher salt. Add chicken on top of rice, and bring to a boil.

5 Lock on the lid, and bring pressure to level 2 (traditional)/high (electric). Reduce heat to low, and cook at 2/high for 10 minutes. Remove from (traditional)/turn off (electric) heat, perform a cold water (traditional)/quick (electric) release, and remove the lid.

6 Remove bay leaf. Stir rice, transfer perloo to a platter, garnish with green onion and flat-leaf parsley, and serve.

NUTRITION PER SERVING

Calories: **370**

Carbohydrates: **37g**

Sugars: **1g**

Dietary fiber: **2g**

Protein: **22g**

Fat: **14g**

Cholesterol: **75mg**

Sodium: **830mg**

Chicken and dumplings is one of the **homiest comfort-food** meals around. Your pressure cooker cooks the dumplings to perfect **tenderness**.

Chicken and **Dumplings**

🍴 6 SERVINGS	🥄 40 MINUTES	🔥 15 MINUTES	⏱ 2/HIGH

INGREDIENTS

1 (3-lb.; 1.5kg) fryer chicken

1 medium leek, white part only, sliced into ½ moons (1 cup)

4 medium carrots, peeled and cut into 1-in. (2.5cm) diagonals (1 cup)

2 medium stalks celery, cut into 1-in. (2.5cm) pieces (½ cup)

2 medium yellow onions, diced large (1½ cups)

1 bay leaf

5 cups homemade or sodium-free chicken stock

2¾ tsp. kosher salt

¾ tsp. freshly ground black pepper

1½ cups all-purpose flour

1 tsp. baking powder

3 TB. shortening

2 large eggs

¾ cup whole milk

1 TB. fresh flat-leaf parsley, minced

METHOD

1 In a 6-quart (5.5l) pressure cooker, combine chicken, leek, carrots, celery, yellow onions, bay leaf, chicken stock, 2 teaspoons kosher salt, and ¼ teaspoon black pepper. Set heat to medium-high (traditional)/ high (electric), and bring to a boil.

2 Lock on the lid, and bring pressure to level 2 (traditional)/high (electric). Reduce heat to low, and cook at 2/high for 5 minutes per 1 pound (.5kg) chicken. Remove from (traditional)/turn off (electric) heat, perform a natural release, and remove the lid.

3 In a large bowl, combine all-purpose flour, remaining ¾ teaspoon kosher salt, baking powder, and shortening until mixture resembles crumbly cornmeal.

4 Add eggs, whole milk, flat-leaf parsley, and remaining ½ teaspoon black pepper, and stir.

5 Transfer chicken to a baking sheet. When cool, remove skin, pull meat off bones, and return meat to the cooker.

6 Set heat to medium-high/high, bring to a boil, and reduce heat to a simmer.

7 Scoop out 1 dumpling, lower to broth level, and gently drop in broth. Repeat with remaining dough, not overlapping dumplings.

8 Set heat to low (traditional)/low (electric). When broth just begins to boil, reduce heat to the lowest possible setting, add the lid but don't lock on, and simmer for 15 minutes. Remove the lid, and push on dumplings. If they're still soft, cover and cook for 5 minutes or until firm.

9 Remove bay leaf. Spoon dumplings into bowls with chicken, vegetables, and broth on top, and serve.

NUTRITION PER SERVING

Calories: 480	Sugars: 6g	Protein: 60g	Cholesterol: 255mg
Carbohydrates: 32g	Dietary fiber: 2g	Fat: 11g	Sodium: 680mg

This is the **Italian version** of chicken cacciatore, made with **mushrooms** plus tomatoes, **red wine,** and **rosemary.**

Chicken **Cacciatore**

6 SERVINGS | 35 MINUTES | 10 MINUTES | 2/HIGH

INGREDIENTS

2½ lb. (1.25kg) bone-in chicken thighs, breasts, and legs (breasts halved crosswise if large)

½ tsp. kosher salt

3 TB. olive oil

8 oz. (225g) cremini or baby bella mushrooms, brushed clean and halved

4 shallots, peeled and halved lengthwise (¾ cup)

3 cloves garlic, chopped (1 TB.)

1 cup dry red wine

1 cup tomato sauce

3 TB. tomato paste

1 tsp. dried rosemary, ground

¼ tsp. freshly ground black pepper

12 oz. (340g) cooked penne pasta, hot

½ cup grated Parmesan cheese

METHOD

1 Season chicken with kosher salt, and set aside for 20 minutes or until salt is absorbed.

2 In a 6-quart (5.5l) pressure cooker set to medium-high (traditional)/high (electric) heat, heat olive oil. When hot, add chicken, skin side down, and brown for 4 minutes. Turn over chicken and brown meat side for 4 minutes. Transfer browned chicken to a plate.

3 Add cremini mushrooms and shallots, and cook for 5 minutes or until they begin to brown.

4 Add garlic, and when it becomes fragrant, add red wine. Reduce wine by half.

5 Return chicken to the cooker along with tomato sauce, tomato paste, rosemary, and black pepper. Bring to a boil, taste, and add more kosher salt as necessary.

6 Lock on the lid, and bring pressure to level 2 (traditional)/high (electric). Reduce heat to low, and cook at 2/high for 10 minutes. Remove from (traditional)/turn off (electric) heat, perform a cold water (traditional)/quick (electric) release, and remove the lid.

7 Stir, taste and adjust seasoning as necessary, and serve over penne pasta with Parmesan cheese on the side.

NUTRITION PER SERVING

Calories: 620	Sugars: 6g	Protein: 36g	Cholesterol: 100mg
Carbohydrates: 53g	Dietary fiber: 2g	Fat: 29g	Sodium: 630mg

Chicken thighs are ideal in **braised** recipes. They stay **tender** and can stand up to the **heavy flavors** of **garlic, peppers,** and **onions** in this dish.

Smothered **Chicken**

4 (2 THIGH + SAUCE) SERVINGS | 30 MINUTES | 12 MINUTES | 2/HIGH

INGREDIENTS

- 2 TB. Spanish paprika
- 1 tsp. garlic powder
- ½ tsp. freshly ground black pepper
- 8 (5-oz.; 140g) bone-in, skin-on chicken thighs
- 2 tsp. kosher salt
- 1½ TB. vegetable oil
- 2 medium yellow onions, thinly sliced (2 cups)
- 1 large green bell pepper, ribs and seeds removed, and thinly sliced (¾ cup)
- 3 medium stalks celery (¾ cup)
- 2 cloves garlic, minced (2 tsp.)
- 2 TB. all-purpose flour
- 1¼ cups water
- 2 medium green onions, chopped (¼ cup)

METHOD

1 In a small bowl, combine Spanish paprika, garlic powder, and black pepper.

2 Season chicken with kosher salt, and sprinkle with spice mix.

3 In a 6-quart (5.5l) pressure cooker set to medium-high (traditional)/high (electric) heat, heat vegetable oil. Add chicken, skin side down, and brown deeply for 4 minutes. Turn over chicken, and brown on other side for 4 minutes. Transfer browned chicken to a tray.

4 Add yellow onions, green bell pepper, and celery to the pressure cooker, and sauté for about 4 minutes or until vegetables wilt.

5 Add garlic and all-purpose flour, stir, and cook for 1 minute.

6 Add water, and bring to a boil.

7 Return chicken to the cooker, and bring to a boil again.

8 Lock on the lid, and bring pressure to level 2 (traditional)/high (electric). Reduce heat to low, and cook at 2/high for 12 minutes. Remove from (traditional)/turn off (electric) heat, perform a cold water (traditional)/quick (electric) release, and remove the lid.

9 Taste, and add more kosher salt as necessary. Transfer chicken to a platter, smother with sauce, top with green onions, and serve.

NUTRITION PER SERVING

Calories: 290	Sugars: 4g	Protein: 33g	Cholesterol: 135mg
Carbohydrates: 11g	Dietary fiber: 2g	Fat: 12g	Sodium: 170mg

40 cloves might seem like a lot of garlic, but it really **mellows** as it cooks under pressure with the **chicken, thyme,** and **seasonings.**

Chicken with 40 Cloves of Garlic

🍴 4 (2 PIECE + SAUCE) SERVINGS	🥄 20 MINUTES	🔥 15 MINUTES	⏱ 2/HIGH

INGREDIENTS

1 (4-lb.; 2kg) whole chicken, cut into 8 pieces (breasts halved crosswise if large)

2 tsp. kosher salt

2 TB. unsalted butter

40 cloves garlic (about 4 heads)

15 sprigs fresh thyme

¼ tsp. freshly ground black pepper

1 cup water

METHOD

1 Season chicken with 1½ teaspoons kosher salt, and set aside until salt is absorbed.

2 In a 4-quart (4l) pressure cooker set to medium-high (traditional)/high (electric) heat, melt unsalted butter. When it foams, add ½ of chicken, skin side down, and brown generously for 4 minutes. Turn over chicken, and brown meat side for 4 minutes. Transfer chicken to a tray, repeat with remaining chicken, and transfer rest of browned chicken to the tray. (Reduce heat if necessary to keep butter from burning.)

3 Add garlic to the cooker, and shake so cloves sink into chicken fat. Add chicken, ½ of thyme sprigs, remaining ½ teaspoon kosher salt, and black pepper. Pour in water, and bring to a boil.

4 Lock on the lid, and bring pressure to level 2 (traditional)/high (electric). Reduce heat to low, and cook at 2/high for 15 minutes. Remove from (traditional)/turn off (electric) heat, perform a cold water (traditional)/quick (electric) release, and remove the lid.

5 Transfer chicken to a platter, and top with garlic cloves and *jus*. Remove thyme leaves from remaining stems, sprinkle leaves over chicken, and serve.

NUTRITION PER SERVING

Calories: **430**	Sugars: **0g**	Protein: **52g**	Cholesterol: **170mg**
Carbohydrates: **10g**	Dietary fiber: **1g**	Fat: **19g**	Sodium: **1,120mg**

Rich with **coconut milk** and exotic from the **green curry paste,** this green curry chicken is far better than any take-out version.

Thai-Style Green Curry Chicken

6 SERVINGS | **30 MINUTES** | **10 MINUTES** | **2/HIGH**

INGREDIENTS

1 TB. vegetable oil

2½ lb. (1.25kg) skinless chicken thighs, legs, and breasts (breasts halved crosswise if large)

1 (1-in; 2.5cm) piece fresh ginger, peeled and minced (1 TB.)

1 TB. minced garlic

3 TB. green curry paste

½ cup homemade or sodium-free chicken stock

3 TB. fish sauce

2 medium carrots, peeled and cut into ¾-in. (2cm) pieces (¾ cup)

1 small red onion, cut into wedges (¾ cup)

4 medium red potatoes, halved (2 cups)

1 (14.5-oz.; 410g) can coconut milk

1 medium zucchini, cut into ¾-in. (1.25cm) rounds

1 medium yellow crookneck squash, cut into ¾-in. (1.25cm) rounds

2 large limes, quartered

Cooked rice noodles or rice, hot

2 serrano chiles, thinly sliced

¼ cup fresh mint leaves, torn

¼ cup fresh Thai basil leaves, torn

¼ cup fresh cilantro leaves

METHOD

1 In a 6-quart (5.5l) pressure cooker set to medium-high (traditional)/high (electric) heat, heat vegetable oil. When hot, add chicken without crowding, and brown on both sides for 4 minutes. (You might need to do this in batches.)

2 Add ginger, garlic, and green curry paste, and stir until spices become aromatic.

3 Add chicken stock, fish sauce, carrots, red onion, and red potatoes. Gently stir, and bring to a boil.

4 Lock on the lid, and bring pressure to level 2 (traditional)/high (electric). Reduce heat to low, and cook at 2/high for 10 minutes. Remove from (traditional)/turn off (electric) heat, perform a cold water (traditional)/quick (electric) release, and remove the lid.

5 Transfer chicken to a platter.

6 Add coconut milk, zucchini, and yellow crookneck squash to the cooker. Set heat to medium (traditional)/high (electric), and simmer for about 5 minutes or until squashes are tender.

7 Pull chicken meat off bones, return chicken to the cooker along with juice of ½ of lime, and stir. Taste, and adjust seasoning as necessary by adding fish sauce and lime juice a little at a time.

8 Serve over hot rice noodles topped with serrano chiles, mint, Thai basil, and cilantro.

NUTRITION PER SERVING

Calories: **510**

Carbohydrates: **30g**

Sugars: **3g**

Dietary fiber: **4g**

Protein: **46g**

Fat: **23g**

Cholesterol: **135mg**

Sodium: **920mg**

For a hotter curry, add another chopped serrano chile along with the chicken.

Red cooked dishes such as this are **simple** and **satisfying,** and they exemplify the flavors of **Chinese food.**

Chinese Red Cooked
Chicken

6 SERVINGS	15 MINUTES	13 MINUTES	2/HIGH

INGREDIENTS

2 whole star anise

1 (3-in.; 7.5cm) cinnamon stick

4 cups homemade or sodium-free vegetable stock

¼ cup soy sauce

1 medium yellow onion, cut into 6 wedges (1 cup)

1 (1-in; 2.5cm) piece fresh ginger, peeled and minced (1 TB.)

1 TB. minced garlic

1 TB. brown sugar

2 TB. Chinese rice wine, dry sherry, or sake

1 (3½-lb.; 1.75kg) whole chicken, cut into 10 pieces (breasts halved crosswise if large)

12 oz. (340g) extra-firm tofu, cut into ½×2×2-in. (1.25×5×5cm) slabs

2 medium carrots, peeled and sliced in ribbons (1½ cups)

1 large green onions, cut into thin rings (¼ cup)

METHOD

1 In a 6-quart (5.5l) pressure cooker, combine star anise, cinnamon stick, vegetable stock, soy sauce, yellow onion, ginger, garlic, brown sugar, and Chinese rice wine. Set heat to medium-high (traditional)/high (electric), and bring to a boil. Reduce heat to a simmer, and cook for 15 minutes.

2 Add chicken, increase heat to medium-high/high, and return to a boil.

3 Lock on the lid, bring pressure to level 2 (traditional)/high (electric), and cook for 13 minutes. Remove from (traditional)/turn off (electric) heat, perform a cold water (traditional)/quick (electric) release, and remove the lid.

4 Add tofu, gently stir into broth, and warm for 5 minutes.

5 Remove cinnamon stick and star anise. Place a piece of chicken and a couple slabs tofu on a plate, ladle hot broth over chicken, and top with carrot ribbons and green onions. Serve with a scoop of hot rice if desired.

NUTRITION PER SERVING

Calories: **610**

Carbohydrates: **17g**

Sugars: **8g**

Dietary fiber: **4g**

Protein: **94g**

Fat: **15g**

Cholesterol: **255mg**

Sodium: **1,020mg**

Originally a herdsman's meal, this **popular comfort food** dish can be made with **beef, pork,** or **lamb.**

Hungarian **Pork Goulash**

| 8 (1 CUP) SERVINGS | 35 MINUTES | 18 MINUTES | 2/HIGH |

INGREDIENTS

2½ lb. (1.25kg) boneless country-style pork ribs, cubed

2½ tsp. kosher salt

1 large red bell pepper, ribs and seeds removed, and thinly sliced (1 cup)

1 medium yellow onion, thinly sliced (1 cup)

3 medium russet potatoes, peeled and cut into 1-in. (2.5cm) chunks (1½ cups)

4 cloves garlic, chopped

2 heaping tsp. paprika

1½ tsp. caraway seeds, crushed

1 tsp. dried marjoram

¼ tsp. freshly ground black pepper

2 TB. red wine vinegar

1½ cups tomato purée

1 cup water

1 TB. fresh flat-leaf parsley, minced

1 cup sour cream

METHOD

1 Season pork ribs with 1½ teaspoons kosher salt, and set aside until salt is absorbed.

2 In a 6-quart (5.5l) pressure cooker set heat to medium-high (traditional)/high (electric), brown ½ of pork cubes on all sides for 4 minutes. Transfer browned pork to a plate, repeat with remaining pork, and transfer rest of browned pork to the plate.

3 Add red bell pepper, yellow onion, russet potatoes, and garlic to the cooker. Stir, and cook for 5 minutes or until vegetables begin to soften.

4 Add browned pork, paprika, caraway seeds, marjoram, black pepper, remaining 1 teaspoon salt, and red wine vinegar, and stir.

5 Stir in tomato purée and water, and bring to a boil.

6 Lock on the lid, bring pressure to level 2 (traditional)/high (electric), and cook for 18 minutes. Remove from (traditional)/turn off (electric) heat, perform your preferred release, and remove the lid.

7 Stir in ½ of flat-leaf parsley.

8 Ladle goulash into bowls, top with a dollop of sour cream and a sprinkle of remaining parsley, and serve.

NUTRITION PER SERVING

Calories: **310**

Carbohydrates: **14g**

Sugars: **5g**

Dietary fiber: **2g**

Protein: **31g**

Fat: **14g**

Cholesterol: **110mg**

Sodium: **920mg**

This pork loin cooks up **juicy** and **tender,** the **Belgian beer** brings another layer of flavor, and the **mustard sauce** is the perfect complement.

Belgian Ale–Braised Pork Loin with Mustard

6 (2 OR 3 SLICE) SERVINGS | 15 MINUTES | 30 MINUTES | 2/HIGH

INGREDIENTS

1 TB. vegetable oil

1 (2½-lb.; 1.75kg) pork loin

½ small yellow onion, minced (⅓ cup)

1 TB. minced garlic

1 pinch kosher salt

½ tsp. freshly ground white pepper

1 cup Belgian farmhouse ale or dry white wine

1 TB. Dusseldorf or Dijon mustard

¼ cup heavy cream (optional)

1 TB. fresh parsley, minced

1 TB. fresh chives, minced

METHOD

1 In a 6-quart (5.5l) pressure cooker set to medium-high (traditional)/ high (electric) heat, heat vegetable oil, gently swirling the pan to coat. When hot, add pork loin and brown on all sides for 5 minutes. (Reduce heat if necessary to keep oil from burning.)

2 Add yellow onion, garlic, kosher salt, and white pepper, and cook for 1 minute or until vegetables begin to soften.

3 Add Belgian farmhouse ale and Dusseldorf mustard, and cook for 2 minutes or until foam subsides and liquid comes to a boil.

4 Lock on the lid, bring pressure to level 2 (traditional)/high (electric), and cook for 30 minutes. Remove from (traditional)/turn off (electric) heat, perform a cold water (traditional)/quick (electric) release, and remove the lid.

5 Transfer pork to a cutting board, and cover with aluminum foil.

6 Return the cooker to medium-high/ high heat, bring sauce to a boil, and cook for 5 minutes or until thickened and reduced by ⅓. Taste, and adjust seasoning as necessary.

7 Add heavy cream (if using), and cook for 2 minutes or until sauce reaches your desired consistency.

8 Slice pork into thin slices, and arrange on a platter. Drizzle sauce over top, garnish with parsley and chives, and serve.

NUTRITION PER SERVING

Calories: 300	Sugars: 0g	Protein: 40g	Cholesterol: 135mg
Carbohydrates: 3g	Dietary fiber: 0g	Fat: 10g	Sodium: 480mg

This Cajun **comfort food** dish features **bell peppers, celery,** and **onions,** the classic **trinity flavor** popular in Louisiana.

Pork **Grillades**

4 STEAKS | **30 MINUTES** | **12 MINUTES** | **2/HIGH**

INGREDIENTS

4 (12-oz.; 340g) bone-in pork butt steaks, cut about ¾ in. (2cm) thick

1 tsp. kosher salt

1 TB. Cajun seasoning or to taste

1 TB. vegetable oil

1 large yellow onion, diced small (1 cup)

½ cup red bell pepper, diced small

½ cup green bell pepper, diced small

2 medium stalks celery, diced small (½ cup)

1¼ cups water or homemade or sodium-free chicken broth

¼ cup tomato sauce

1 TB. Worcestershire sauce

Hot sauce

METHOD

1 Season pork butt steaks on both sides with kosher salt followed by Cajun seasoning, and set aside until seasonings are absorbed.

2 In a 6-quart (5.5l) pressure cooker set to medium-high (traditional)/ high (electric) heat, heat vegetable oil. When hot, add pork, in batches or one at a time, and sear for 4 minutes or until seasoning begins to blacken. Transfer seared pork to a plate, and repeat with remaining pork, transferring rest of browned pork to the plate. (Reduce heat if necessary to keep oil from burning.)

3 Add yellow onion, red bell pepper, green bell pepper, and celery to the cooker, and sauté for 3 minutes or until vegetables begin to soften.

4 Return pork to the cooker. Add water, tomato sauce, and Worcestershire sauce, and bring to a boil.

5 Lock on the lid, bring pressure to level 2 (traditional)/high (electric), and cook for 12 minutes. Remove from (traditional)/turn off (electric) heat, perform a quick release, and remove the lid.

6 Serve with hot sauce on the side.

NUTRITION PER SERVING

Calories: 290	Sugars: 3g	Protein: 38g	Cholesterol: 125mg
Carbohydrates: 4g	Dietary fiber: 1g	Fat: 12g	Sodium: 1,180mg

This pulled pork is **tender, succulent,** and **juicy** and cooks quickly, thanks to your pressure cooker.

Southern-Style **Pulled Pork**

| 6 (½ CUP) SERVINGS | 10 MINUTES + CURE TIME | 45 MINUTES | 2/HIGH |

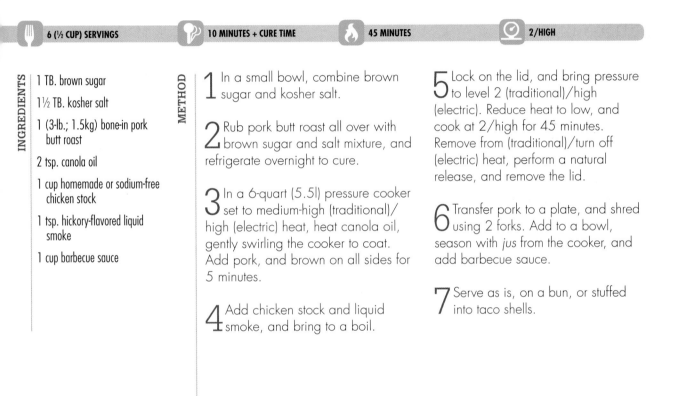

INGREDIENTS

1 TB. brown sugar

1½ TB. kosher salt

1 (3-lb.; 1.5kg) bone-in pork butt roast

2 tsp. canola oil

1 cup homemade or sodium-free chicken stock

1 tsp. hickory-flavored liquid smoke

1 cup barbecue sauce

METHOD

1 In a small bowl, combine brown sugar and kosher salt.

2 Rub pork butt roast all over with brown sugar and salt mixture, and refrigerate overnight to cure.

3 In a 6-quart (5.5l) pressure cooker set to medium-high (traditional)/high (electric) heat, heat canola oil, gently swirling the cooker to coat. Add pork, and brown on all sides for 5 minutes.

4 Add chicken stock and liquid smoke, and bring to a boil.

5 Lock on the lid, and bring pressure to level 2 (traditional)/high (electric). Reduce heat to low, and cook at 2/high for 45 minutes. Remove from (traditional)/turn off (electric) heat, perform a natural release, and remove the lid.

6 Transfer pork to a plate, and shred using 2 forks. Add to a bowl, season with *jus* from the cooker, and add barbecue sauce.

7 Serve as is, on a bun, or stuffed into taco shells.

NUTRITION PER SERVING

| Calories: 310 | Sugars: 14g | Protein: 31g | Cholesterol: 100mg |
| Carbohydrates: 17g | Dietary fiber: 0g | Fat: 12g | Sodium: 1,920mg |

This wonderful **Indian stew** blends **sweet** and **sour** flavors. Increase the **spice** if you like by adding a **dried hot chile** or two while the stew cooks.

Pork **Vindaloo**

6 (⅔ CUP) SERVINGS	30 MINUTES + MARINATE TIME	25 MINUTES	2/HIGH

INGREDIENTS

2 lb. (1kg) country-style pork ribs, cut into 1-in. (2.5cm) cubes

½ tsp ground coriander

½ tsp. ground cumin

½ tsp. ground mustard seeds

¼ tsp. ground cloves

½ tsp. turmeric

1 tsp. kosher salt

⅓ cup white vinegar

¼ cup vegetable oil

2 medium yellow onions, chopped (1½ cups)

3 TB. minced garlic

1 cup tomato sauce

1 TB. brown sugar

1 small red onion, thinly sliced (½ cup)

2 large limes, 1 quartered and 1 halved

2 medium green onions, sliced into thin rings (⅓ cup)

⅓ cup fresh cilantro, coarsely chopped

1 Fresno or jalapeño chile, sliced

METHOD

1 In a large bowl, combine pork, coriander, cumin, mustard seeds, cloves, turmeric, and kosher salt. Add white vinegar, and stir to combine. Set aside for 1 hour, or refrigerate for up to 6 hours.

2 Drain pork, and reserve marinade.

3 In a 6-quart (5.5l) pressure cooker set to medium-high (traditional)/high (electric) heat, heat vegetable oil. Add pork, and brown generously on all sides for 5 minutes. Transfer browned pork to the large bowl.

4 Add yellow onions to the cooker, and cook for 3 or 4 minutes to soften.

5 Add garlic, and cook for 30 seconds or until fragrant.

6 Add tomato sauce, pork, reserved marinade, and brown sugar. Stir to combine, and bring to a boil.

7 Lock on the lid, and bring pressure to level 2 (traditional)/high (electric). Reduce heat to low, and cook at 2/high for 25 minutes. Remove from (traditional)/turn off (electric) heat, perform a quick release, and remove the lid.

8 In a small bowl, place red onion. Squeeze juice from halved lime over top, and toss to combine.

9 Stir stew, taste, and add more kosher salt as necessary. Serve topped with 1 lime wedge, pickled red onions, green onions, cilantro, and Fresno chile.

NUTRITION PER SERVING

Calories: 330	Sugars: 6g	Protein: 31g	Cholesterol: 100mg
Carbohydrates: 10g	Dietary fiber: 2g	Fat: 19g	Sodium: 730mg

This traditional Mexican stew features **yellow hominy,** a corn-based ingredient. If you can find **Mexican oregano,** use it for a more authentic flavor.

Pork **Posole**

6 (⅔ CUP) SERVINGS | 40 MINUTES | 20 MINUTES | 2/HIGH

INGREDIENTS

- 1 lb. (450g) tomatillos, outer paper skins removed
- 2 TB. lard or olive oil
- 1 (2½-lb.; 1.25kg) pork shoulder, cut into 1-in. (2.5cm) cubes
- 1 medium yellow onion, diced small (1 cup)
- ¼ cup coarsely chopped garlic
- 2 tsp. dried oregano
- 1 TB. dark chili powder
- 1 TB. tomato paste
- 1 tsp. kosher salt
- ¼ tsp. freshly ground black pepper
- Water
- 1 (14.5-oz.; 410g) can yellow hominy
- ¼ cup fresh cilantro, chopped

METHOD

1 Preheat the broiler.

2 Place tomatillos on a baking sheet, and broil for 4 minutes or until blackened. Turn over, and blacken other side. (Tomatillos will wilt and collapse on themselves.)

3 In a 4-quart (4l) pressure cooker set to medium-high (traditional)/high (electric) heat, heat lard. When hot, add ½ of pork. Brown on all sides for 4 minutes, transfer browned pork to a plate, repeat with remaining pork, and transfer rest of browned pork to the plate. (Reduce heat if necessary to avoid burning.)

4 Add yellow onion to the cooker, stir, and cook for about 5 minutes or until it wilts.

5 Add tomatillos and their juice, garlic, oregano, dark chili powder, and tomato paste, and stir.

6 Return pork and its juice to the cooker, and add kosher salt and black pepper. Add enough water to come up to top edge of meat, and bring to a boil.

7 Lock on the lid, bring pressure to level 2 (traditional)/high (electric), and cook for 15 minutes. Turn off heat, let pork sit for 5 minutes, perform a quick release, and remove the lid.

8 Add yellow hominy and cilantro, set heat to medium (traditional)/ high (electric), and cook for 4 minutes or until hominy is warm. Taste, and adjust kosher salt and pepper as necessary.

9 Serve in bowls alongside fresh cilantro and your favorite toppings (like shredded cabbage, lime wedges, thinly sliced red onion, sour cream, and shredded Monterey jack cheese).

NUTRITION PER SERVING

Calories: 610	Sugars: 5g	Protein: 48g	Cholesterol: 135mg
Carbohydrates: 63g	Dietary fiber: 6g	Fat: 20g	Sodium: 530mg

This one-dish meal is **hearty** and **filling**. The recipe comes together surprisingly **fast** in your pressure cooker and doesn't require a lot of cleanup.

One-Pot Sausage, Potatoes, and Greens

4 (1½ CUP) SERVINGS	15 MINUTES	10 MINUTES	2/HIGH

INGREDIENTS

- 1½ cups homemade or sodium-free vegetable or chicken broth
- ½ tsp. crushed red pepper flakes (optional)
- ¾ tsp. kosher salt
- 8 cups mixed collard, turnip, kale, and mustard greens, stems removed and chopped
- 8 medium red potatoes, skin on and scrubbed
- 2 (8-oz.; 225g) smoked sausages or kielbasa
- Freshly ground black pepper

METHOD

1 In a 6-quart (5.5l) pressure cooker, combine vegetable broth, crushed red pepper flakes (if using), and ½ teaspoon kosher salt. Set heat to medium-high (traditional)/high (electric), and bring to a boil.

2 Add mixed greens, and using a pair of tongs, turn greens to coat with broth.

3 Place red potatoes on top of greens, and add sausage on top of potatoes. Season with remaining ¼ teaspoon kosher salt, and bring to a boil.

4 Lock on the lid, and bring pressure to level 2 (traditional)/high (electric). Reduce heat to low, and cook at 2/high for 10 minutes. Remove from (traditional)/turn off (electric) heat, perform a cold water (traditional)/quick (electric) release, and remove the lid.

5 Spoon greens and some broth onto a platter, and top with potatoes.

6 Cut sausages into serving-size pieces, and arrange among potatoes. Season with a few grinds of black pepper, and serve.

NUTRITION PER SERVING

Calories: **570**	Sugars: **6g**	Protein: **20g**	Cholesterol: **75mg**
Carbohydrates: **53g**	Dietary fiber: **7g**	Fat: **31g**	Sodium: **1,530mg**

This **delicious, deeply flavored fish** dish is light and comes together quickly and easily.

Asian Steamed **Fish**

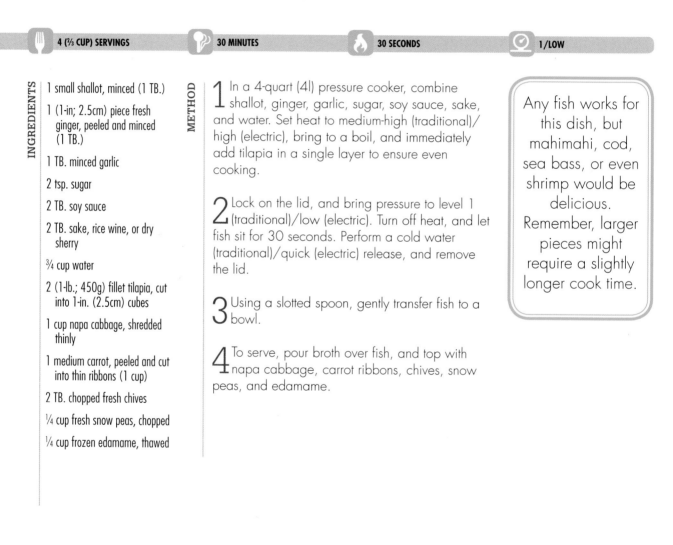

4 (⅔ CUP) SERVINGS | **30 MINUTES** | **30 SECONDS** | **1/LOW**

INGREDIENTS

1 small shallot, minced (1 TB.)

1 (1-in; 2.5cm) piece fresh ginger, peeled and minced (1 TB.)

1 TB. minced garlic

2 tsp. sugar

2 TB. soy sauce

2 TB. sake, rice wine, or dry sherry

¾ cup water

2 (1-lb.; 450g) fillet tilapia, cut into 1-in. (2.5cm) cubes

1 cup napa cabbage, shredded thinly

1 medium carrot, peeled and cut into thin ribbons (1 cup)

2 TB. chopped fresh chives

¼ cup fresh snow peas, chopped

¼ cup frozen edamame, thawed

METHOD

1 In a 4-quart (4l) pressure cooker, combine shallot, ginger, garlic, sugar, soy sauce, sake, and water. Set heat to medium-high (traditional)/ high (electric), bring to a boil, and immediately add tilapia in a single layer to ensure even cooking.

2 Lock on the lid, and bring pressure to level 1 (traditional)/low (electric). Turn off heat, and let fish sit for 30 seconds. Perform a cold water (traditional)/quick (electric) release, and remove the lid.

3 Using a slotted spoon, gently transfer fish to a bowl.

4 To serve, pour broth over fish, and top with napa cabbage, carrot ribbons, chives, snow peas, and edamame.

Any fish works for this dish, but mahimahi, cod, sea bass, or even shrimp would be delicious. Remember, larger pieces might require a slightly longer cook time.

NUTRITION PER SERVING

| Calories: 270 | Sugars: 4g | Protein: 48g | Cholesterol: 115mg |
| Carbohydrates: 7g | Dietary fiber: 1g | Fat: 4.5g | Sodium: 790mg |

This recipe is very **simple to prepare,** thanks to your pressure cooker. Use **fresh, good-quality** ingredients to produce a **delicious final dish.**

Salmon en Papillote

🍴 2 (1 FILET) SERVINGS	💧 30 MINUTES	🔥 7 MINUTES	⏲ 2/HIGH

INGREDIENTS

2 (7-oz.; 200g) fillets salmon

½ tsp. kosher salt

⅛ tsp. freshly ground black pepper

1 small stalk celery, diced small (¼ cup)

5 thin slices yellow onion (¼ cup)

1 medium carrot, peeled and cut into paper-thin rounds (½ cup)

2 slices lemon

2 tsp. fresh flat-leaf parsley, minced

METHOD

1 Add a steamer basket to a 4-quart (4l) pressure cooker, and fill with the minimum amount of water allowed for your cooker.

2 Place a 10×10-inch (25×25cm) piece of aluminum foil on your counter, and drizzle 1 teaspoon olive oil over top. Place salmon on the foil with a bit of space between fillets.

3 Season salmon on both sides with kosher salt and black pepper. Scatter celery, yellow onion, and carrot over salmon, and top each piece with 1 lemon slice.

4 Place another 10×10-inch (25×25cm) piece of foil on top of the first, and crimp tightly at the edges. Add foil packet to the steamer basket, set heat to medium-high (traditional)/high (electric), and bring to a boil.

5 Lock on the lid, bring pressure to level 2 (traditional)/high (electric), and cook for 7 minutes. Remove from (traditional)/turn off (electric) heat, perform a cold water (traditional)/quick (electric) release, and remove the lid.

6 Transfer foil packet to a plate, carry to the table, and open the packet tableside for a bit of flourish. Serve topped with vegetables and garnished with flat-leaf parsley.

NUTRITION PER SERVING

Calories: 510	Sugars: 3g	Protein: 40g	Cholesterol: 100mg
Carbohydrates: 6g	Dietary fiber: 2g	Fat: 35g	Sodium: 610mg

The **spicy Indian sauce** in this quick and easy fish dish is **incredible** and **complements** the tilapia quite nicely.

Fish **Curry**

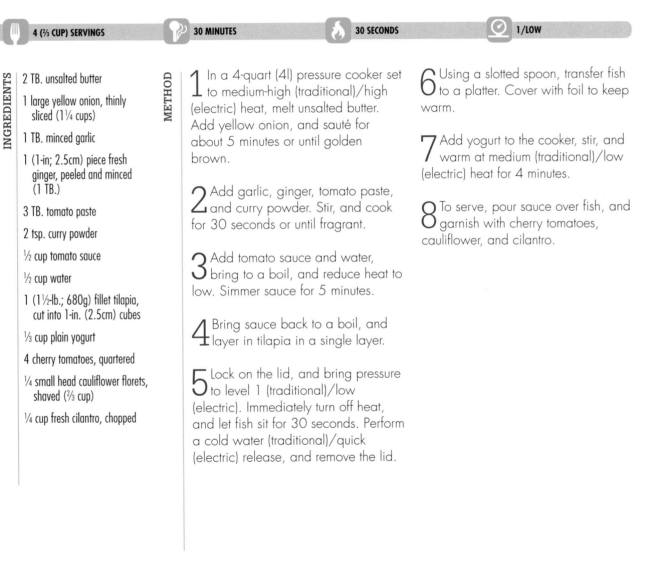

4 (⅔ CUP) SERVINGS | **30 MINUTES** | **30 SECONDS** | **1/LOW**

INGREDIENTS

- 2 TB. unsalted butter
- 1 large yellow onion, thinly sliced (1¼ cups)
- 1 TB. minced garlic
- 1 (1-in; 2.5cm) piece fresh ginger, peeled and minced (1 TB.)
- 3 TB. tomato paste
- 2 tsp. curry powder
- ½ cup tomato sauce
- ½ cup water
- 1 (1½-lb.; 680g) fillet tilapia, cut into 1-in. (2.5cm) cubes
- ⅓ cup plain yogurt
- 4 cherry tomatoes, quartered
- ¼ small head cauliflower florets, shaved (⅔ cup)
- ¼ cup fresh cilantro, chopped

METHOD

1 In a 4-quart (4l) pressure cooker set to medium-high (traditional)/high (electric) heat, melt unsalted butter. Add yellow onion, and sauté for about 5 minutes or until golden brown.

2 Add garlic, ginger, tomato paste, and curry powder. Stir, and cook for 30 seconds or until fragrant.

3 Add tomato sauce and water, bring to a boil, and reduce heat to low. Simmer sauce for 5 minutes.

4 Bring sauce back to a boil, and layer in tilapia in a single layer.

5 Lock on the lid, and bring pressure to level 1 (traditional)/low (electric). Immediately turn off heat, and let fish sit for 30 seconds. Perform a cold water (traditional)/quick (electric) release, and remove the lid.

6 Using a slotted spoon, transfer fish to a platter. Cover with foil to keep warm.

7 Add yogurt to the cooker, stir, and warm at medium (traditional)/low (electric) heat for 4 minutes.

8 To serve, pour sauce over fish, and garnish with cherry tomatoes, cauliflower, and cilantro.

NUTRITION PER SERVING

Calories: **270**	Sugars: **5g**	Protein: **37g**	Cholesterol: **100mg**
Carbohydrates: **11g**	Dietary fiber: **3g**	Fat: **9g**	Sodium: **220mg**

This recipe is a fantastic **blend of spice** and **seafood.** Serve with rice to soak up all the **delicious** sauce.

Thai Steamed **Mussels**

4 (2 CUP) SERVINGS	15 MINUTES	1 MINUTE	1/LOW

INGREDIENTS

4 lb. (2kg) mussels, rinsed

3 cloves garlic, minced (1 TB.)

1 tsp. cumin seed, crushed

3 TB. red curry paste

1½ TB. Madras curry powder

1 (10-oz.; 400ml) can coconut milk

1 (8-oz.; 262.5ml) bottle clam juice

1 TB. sugar

½ tsp. turmeric

3 TB. fish sauce

1 TB. freshly squeezed lime juice

1 TB. tomato paste

½ medium yellow onion, diced fine (¼ cup)

½ cup fresh cilantro

2 serrano chiles, thinly sliced

2 medium green onions, white and green parts, sliced into thin rings (¼ cup)

1 medium lime, quartered

METHOD

1 Squeeze mussels, and discard any that don't close. Set aside.

2 In a 6-quart (5.5l) pressure cooker, combine garlic, cumin, red curry paste, Madras curry powder, coconut milk, clam juice, sugar, turmeric, fish sauce, lime juice, tomato paste, and yellow onion. Set heat to medium-high (traditional)/high (electric), and bring to a boil, whisking to break up any curry paste clumps.

3 Add mussels, and return to a boil.

4 Lock on the lid, bring pressure to level 1 (traditional)/low (electric), and cook for 1 minute. Remove from (traditional)/turn off (electric) heat, perform a cold water (traditional)/quick (electric) release, and remove the lid.

5 Stir mussels to coat in broth.

6 Using a slotted spoon, transfer mussels to a deep platter. Pour broth over top, and garnish with cilantro, serrano chiles, and green onions. Serve with lime wedges on the side.

NUTRITION PER SERVING

Calories: **560**

Carbohydrates: **26g**

Sugars: **5g**

Dietary fiber: **1g**

Protein: **57g**

Fat: **25g**

Cholesterol: **130mg**

Sodium: **2,500mg**

This recipe produces **seasoned, beer-steamed** shrimp with **East Coast** flavors plus a **little heat** for good measure.

Beer-Steamed **Shrimp**

4 (14 SHRIMP) SERVINGS	10 MINUTES	2 MINUTES	2/HIGH

INGREDIENTS

1½ cups American lager

1 TB. pickling spice

3 TB. minced garlic

1 tsp. hot sauce

2 lb. (1kg.) shell-on shrimp (size 26 to 30), thawed

1 TB. fresh flat-leaf parsley, minced

1 TB. Old Bay seasoning

METHOD

1 In a 6-quart (5.5l) pressure cooker, combine American lager, pickling spice, garlic, and hot sauce. Set heat to medium-high (traditional)/high (electric), and bring to a boil.

2 Add shrimp, and return to a boil.

3 Lock on the lid, bring pressure to level 2 (traditional)/high (electric), and cook for 2 minutes. Remove from (traditional)/turn off (electric) heat, perform a cold water (traditional)/quick (electric) release, and remove the lid.

4 Transfer shrimp to a bowl, and ladle some broth over top. Sprinkle flat-leaf parsley and Old Bay seasoning over top, and serve immediately with lots of cocktail sauce or remoulade.

> If you can't find Old Bay seasoning, you can substitute any Cajun-style seasoning you like.

NUTRITION PER SERVING

Calories: 290	Sugars: 0g	Protein: 47g	Cholesterol: 350mg
Carbohydrates: 7g	Dietary fiber: 0g	Fat: 4g	Sodium: 410mg

This **homey, one-pot dish** full of shrimp, chicken, vegetables, and rice makes a quick, comforting meal.

Cajun-Style Shrimp **Jambalaya**

6 SERVINGS   **35 MINUTES**   **5 MINUTES**   **2/HIGH**

INGREDIENTS

6 (5-oz.; 140g) chicken thighs

1 tsp. kosher salt

1 TB. vegetable oil

1 medium yellow onion, diced small (1 cup)

2 large stalks celery, diced small (½ cup)

1 small green bell pepper, ribs and seeds removed, and diced small (½ cup)

1 TB. minced garlic

1½ cups long-grain rice

1 bay leaf

½ tsp. dried thyme

2 cups homemade or sodium-free chicken or vegetable broth

1 cup crushed tomatoes, with juice

1 lb. (450g) raw shrimp (size 31 to 35), thawed if frozen, peeled, deveined, and drained

1 TB. fresh flat-leaf parsley, minced

METHOD

1 Season chicken thighs with ½ teaspoon kosher salt on all sides, and set aside until salt is absorbed.

2 In a 6-quart (5.5l) pressure cooker set to medium-high (traditional)/high (electric) heat, heat vegetable oil. When hot, add chicken, skin side down, and brown deeply on both sides for 4 minutes. Transfer to a plate.

3 Add yellow onion, celery, and green bell pepper to the cooker. Stir, and cook for about 3 minutes or until vegetables soften.

4 Add garlic, and cook for 30 seconds or until fragrant.

5 Add long-grain rice, bay leaf, and thyme, and stir to coat. Add chicken broth, crushed tomatoes with juice, and remaining ½ teaspoon kosher salt. Swirl the cooker to distribute rice, and nestle chicken on top. Bring to a boil.

6 Lock on the lid, bring pressure to level 2 (traditional)/high (electric), and cook for 5 minutes. Remove from (traditional)/turn off (electric) heat, perform a cold water (traditional)/quick (electric) release, and remove the lid.

7 Layer shrimp on top of rice, put lid back on, and cook for 6 minutes.

8 Remove bay leaf. Stir in flat-leaf parsley, and serve hot.

NUTRITION PER SERVING

Calories: **380**

Carbohydrates: **42g**

Sugars: **3g**

Dietary fiber: **3g**

Protein: **37g**

Fat: **6g**

Cholesterol: **185mg**

Sodium: **490mg**

rice, grains, and **breads**

Rice and grains are well suited to pressure cooking, but so are many breads, especially quick breads. There's no better way to cook cornbread, and steamed brown bread will soon become a suppertime staple.

The **natural, nutty** flavor of basmati rice becomes **sweet** when paired with **yellow onion** in this recipe, and the **peas** add color and texture.

Basmati Rice **Pilaf**

🍴 4 (½ CUP) SERVINGS	🫗 15 MINUTES	🔥 5 MINUTES	⏲ 2/HIGH

INGREDIENTS

1 TB. unsalted butter

1 medium yellow onion, diced small (½ cup)

1 cup basmati rice

2 cups water

¾ cup frozen peas

METHOD

1 In a 4-quart (4l) pressure cooker set to medium (traditional)/high (electric) heat, melt unsalted butter.

2 Add yellow onion, and cook for 8 minutes or until caramelized and brown.

3 Add basmati rice and water, stir gently, and bring to a boil.

4 Lock on the lid, and bring pressure to level 2 (traditional)/high (electric). Reduce heat to low, and cook at 2/high for 5 minutes. Remove from (traditional)/turn off (electric) heat, perform a quick release, and remove the lid.

5 Add peas, and stir with a fork to fluff rice and mix in peas. Place the lid back on the cooker, and let pilaf sit for at least 8 minutes to cook peas. Serve hot.

For an authentic Spanish side dish, add some saffron. Or stir in a pinch of cardamom and some almonds and serve alongside an Indian curry.

NUTRITION PER SERVING

Calories: 210	Sugars: 4g	Protein: 5g	Cholesterol: 10mg
Carbohydrates: 41g	Dietary fiber: 3g	Fat: 3.5g	Sodium: 480mg

Reminiscent of **Cajun dirty rice,** this **hearty** lentils and oats dish is **wonderful** served alongside chicken or any braised or roasted meat entrée.

Dirty Oats with Lentils

🍴 4 (1 CUP) SERVINGS	🥄 15 MINUTES	🔥 12 MINUTES	⏱ 2/HIGH

INGREDIENTS

1½ TB. vegetable oil

1 large yellow onion, diced small (1¼ cups)

1 TB. minced garlic

½ tsp. kosher salt

¾ cup whole or steel-cut oats

¾ cup du Puy lentils

1 TB. dried sage

¾ tsp. freshly ground black pepper

¼ tsp. allspice

⅛ tsp. ground nutmeg

3 cups homemade or sodium-free vegetable broth

METHOD

1 In a 4-quart (4l) pressure cooker set to medium-high (traditional)/high (electric) heat, heat vegetable oil. Add yellow onion, and sauté for about 3 minutes or until soft.

2 Add garlic, and cook for 30 seconds or until fragrant.

3 Add kosher salt, whole oats, du Puy lentils, sage, black pepper, allspice, and nutmeg, and stir to coat. Add vegetable broth, and bring to a boil.

4 Lock on the lid, and bring pressure to level 2 (traditional)/high (electric). Reduce heat to low, and cook at 2/high for 12 minutes. Remove from (traditional)/turn off (electric) heat, perform a cold water (traditional)/quick (electric) release, and remove the lid.

5 Stir, taste and add seasoning as necessary, and serve.

NUTRITION PER SERVING

Calories: 250	Sugars: 4g	Protein: 10g	Cholesterol: 0mg
Carbohydrates: 38g	Dietary fiber: 8g	Fat: 7g	Sodium: 350mg

The **nuttiness** of wild rice is enhanced by the flavors of **shallots** and **parsley** in this quick and easy dish.

Wild **Rice**

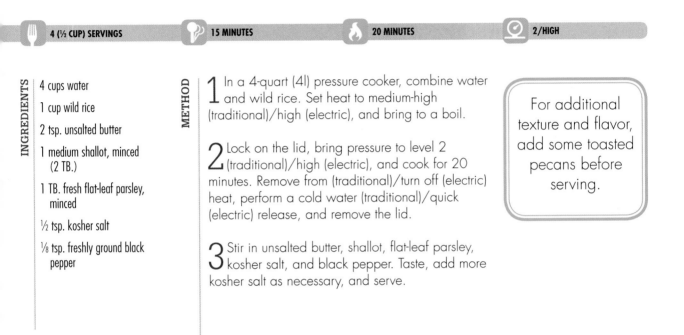

| 4 (½ CUP) SERVINGS | 15 MINUTES | 20 MINUTES | 2/HIGH |

INGREDIENTS

- 4 cups water
- 1 cup wild rice
- 2 tsp. unsalted butter
- 1 medium shallot, minced (2 TB.)
- 1 TB. fresh flat-leaf parsley, minced
- ½ tsp. kosher salt
- ⅛ tsp. freshly ground black pepper

METHOD

1 In a 4-quart (4l) pressure cooker, combine water and wild rice. Set heat to medium-high (traditional)/high (electric), and bring to a boil.

2 Lock on the lid, bring pressure to level 2 (traditional)/high (electric), and cook for 20 minutes. Remove from (traditional)/turn off (electric) heat, perform a cold water (traditional)/quick (electric) release, and remove the lid.

3 Stir in unsalted butter, shallot, flat-leaf parsley, kosher salt, and black pepper. Taste, add more kosher salt as necessary, and serve.

> For additional texture and flavor, add some toasted pecans before serving.

NUTRITION PER SERVING

| Calories: **160** | Sugars: **1g** | Protein: **6g** | Cholesterol: **5mg** |
| Carbohydrates: **31g** | Dietary fiber: **3g** | Fat: **2.5g** | Sodium: **240mg** |

In this risotto, **crisp asparagus** and **sun-dried tomatoes** pair perfectly with creamy rice.

Asparagus and Sun-Dried Tomato **Risotto**

🍴 4 (⅔ CUP) SERVINGS	👐 20 MINUTES	🔥 7 MINUTES	⏱ 1/LOW

INGREDIENTS

2 TB. olive oil

2 thin slices prosciutto

1 TB. minced garlic

1 cup arborio rice

¼ cup dry white wine

3 cups homemade or sodium-free vegetable stock

12 spears asparagus, tips left whole and stems cut into thin rounds (¾ cup)

⅓ cup sun-dried tomatoes in oil, drained and chopped

2 TB. unsalted butter

½ cup grated Parmesan cheese

1 TB. fresh chives, minced

METHOD

1 In a 4-quart (4l) pressure cooker set to medium-high (traditional)/high (electric) heat, heat olive oil. Lay prosciutto in oil as if you were frying bacon, and cook on both sides for 3 minutes or until brown and crispy. Transfer prosciutto to a paper towel–lined plate.

2 Add garlic to the pressure cooker, and sauté for about 15 seconds or until aromatic. Add arborio rice, and stir to coat.

3 Add dry white wine, and burn off alcohol for about 30 seconds. Add vegetable stock, and bring to a boil.

4 Lock on the lid, bring pressure to level 1 (traditional)/low (electric), and cook for 7 minutes. Remove from (traditional)/turn off (electric) heat, perform a cold water (traditional)/quick (electric) release, and remove the lid.

5 Meanwhile, chop prosciutto into crumbles.

6 Add asparagus, sun-dried tomatoes, unsalted butter, and Parmesan cheese to the cooker, and stir. Taste, and add more kosher salt as necessary.

7 Serve topped with prosciutto crumbles and chives.

NUTRITION PER SERVING

Calories: 400	Sugars: 5g	Protein: 13g	Cholesterol: 30mg	
Carbohydrates: 45g	Dietary fiber: 4g	Fat: 18g	Sodium: 610mg	

In this recipe, your pressure cooker produces a **creamy, brothy, flavorful risotto** quickly and without fuss.

Risotto **Milanese**

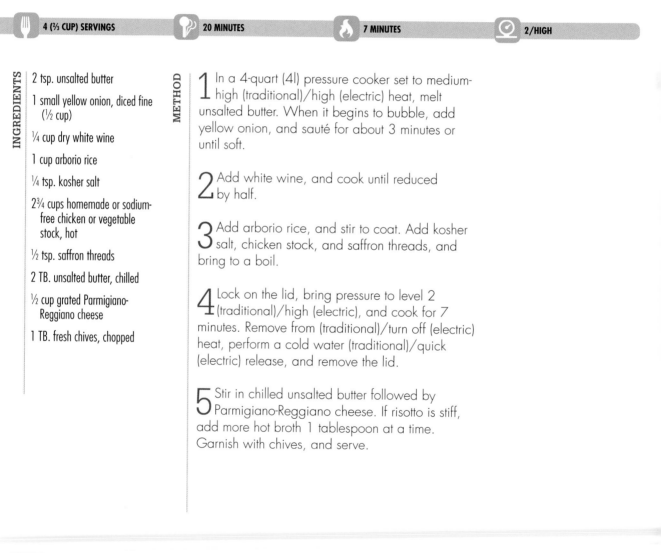

4 (⅔ CUP) SERVINGS　　　20 MINUTES　　　7 MINUTES　　　2/HIGH

INGREDIENTS

2 tsp. unsalted butter

1 small yellow onion, diced fine (½ cup)

¼ cup dry white wine

1 cup arborio rice

¼ tsp. kosher salt

2¾ cups homemade or sodium-free chicken or vegetable stock, hot

½ tsp. saffron threads

2 TB. unsalted butter, chilled

½ cup grated Parmigiano-Reggiano cheese

1 TB. fresh chives, chopped

METHOD

1 In a 4-quart (4l) pressure cooker set to medium-high (traditional)/high (electric) heat, melt unsalted butter. When it begins to bubble, add yellow onion, and sauté for about 3 minutes or until soft.

2 Add white wine, and cook until reduced by half.

3 Add arborio rice, and stir to coat. Add kosher salt, chicken stock, and saffron threads, and bring to a boil.

4 Lock on the lid, bring pressure to level 2 (traditional)/high (electric), and cook for 7 minutes. Remove from (traditional)/turn off (electric) heat, perform a cold water (traditional)/quick (electric) release, and remove the lid.

5 Stir in chilled unsalted butter followed by Parmigiano-Reggiano cheese. If risotto is stiff, add more hot broth 1 tablespoon at a time. Garnish with chives, and serve.

NUTRITION PER SERVING

Calories: 320　　Sugars: 1g　　Protein: 11g　　Cholesterol: 40mg

Carbohydrates: 39g　　Dietary fiber: 1g　　Fat: 12g　　Sodium: 660mg

Coconut milk gives this gluten-free rice dish an exotic flavor, and black-eyed peas keep it earthy.

Jamaican-Style Rice and Peas

| 4 (⅔ CUP) SERVINGS | 4 MINUTES | 5 MINUTES | 2/HIGH |

INGREDIENTS

1 cup medium-grain rice

1 cup water

1 cup coconut milk

¼ tsp. kosher salt

½ cup black-eyed or pigeon peas, washed, picked over, soaked overnight, and drained

¼ cup fresh cilantro, minced

2 medium green onions, chopped (¼ cup)

METHOD

1 In a 4-quart (4l) pressure cooker, combine medium-grain rice, water, coconut milk, kosher salt, and black-eyed peas. Set heat to medium-high (traditional)/high (electric), and bring to a boil.

2 Lock on the lid, bring pressure to level 2 (traditional)/high (electric), and cook for 5 minutes. Remove from (traditional)/turn off (electric) heat, perform a cold water (traditional)/quick (electric) release, and remove the lid.

3 Fluff rice with a fork, add cilantro and green onions, fluff again, and serve.

For a Cuban-style one-pot meal, use black beans instead of the black-eyed peas and add some ham, sausage, or both.

NUTRITION PER SERVING

| Calories: 340 | Sugars: 0g | Protein: 8g | Cholesterol: 0mg |
| Carbohydrates: 49g | Dietary fiber: 5g | Fat: 13g | Sodium: 220mg |

This **slightly sweet** brown bread is great at breakfast with a bit of **butter** and fruit jam, especially Swedish lingonberry jam.

Steamed Brown Bread
with Raisins

🍴 1 (10-SLICE) LOAF	🥄 20 MINUTES	🔥 40 MINUTES	⏲ 2/HIGH

INGREDIENTS

1 cup whole-wheat flour

½ cup cornmeal

½ tsp. baking powder

½ tsp. baking soda

½ tsp. kosher salt

1 cup buttermilk

½ cup molasses

⅓ cup raisins

METHOD

1 In a large bowl, combine whole-wheat flour, cornmeal, baking powder, baking soda, and kosher salt. Add buttermilk and molasses, and stir gently to combine. Stir in raisins.

2 Butter the inside of an asparagus can with one open end, and add dough to the can, tapping it on the counter as you go to avoid any large air bubbles in dough. When all dough is in the can, gently push down on dough with a spoon and jiggle the can to remove more bubbles. Place a piece of aluminum foil over the top of the can, and secure it tightly with a rubber band.

3 Add a trivet to the bottom of a 8-quart (7.5l) pressure cooker (be sure the can will fit inside with the lid on), and fill with the minimum amount of water allowed for your cooker. Set heat to medium-high (traditional)/high (electric), and bring to a boil.

4 Lock on the lid, and bring pressure to level 2 (traditional)/high (electric), and cook for 40 minutes. Remove from (traditional)/turn off (electric) heat, let bread sit for 5 minutes, perform a quick release, and remove the lid.

5 Transfer the can to a cooling rack, and cool completely before removing bread from the can.

6 Slice, and serve.

NUTRITION PER SERVING

Calories: 150

Carbohydrates: 33g

Sugars: 14g

Dietary fiber: 2g

Protein: 3g

Fat: 0g

Cholesterol: 0mg

Sodium: 220mg

I use an empty asparagus can as my bread pan; two buttered soup cans would work, too. Just be sure one end is open and the other is closed.

If you don't like crusty bread, this recipe is for you. This crust-free bread is **buttery, soft,** and **yeasty,** perfect for grilled cheese sandwiches.

Crustless **Sandwich Bread**

🍴 1 (10-SLICE) LOAF	🥄 1 HOUR + RISE TIME	🔥 20 MINUTES	⏱ 2/HIGH

INGREDIENTS

7 fl. oz. (205ml) warm (90°F; 32°C) water

½ tsp. instant yeast

½ tsp. sugar

½ tsp. nonfat dry milk powder

¼ tsp. kosher salt

1½ cups bread flour, plus more for dusting

1 tsp. unsalted butter, softened

NUTRITION PER SERVING

Calories: 130
Carbohydrates: 25g
Sugars: 0g
Dietary fiber: 1g
Protein: 4g
Fat: 1g
Cholesterol: 0mg
Sodium: 0mg

METHOD

1 Add a trivet to a 6-quart (5.5l) pressure cooker, and fill with the minimum amount of water allowed for your cooker. Butter a 6-cup heatproof container.

2 In a large bowl, whisk together warm water, instant yeast, sugar, dry milk powder, and kosher salt. Let mixture sit for 5 minutes or until milk powder dissolves.

3 Add bread flour and softened unsalted butter, and using a wooden spoon, mix dough by moving the spoon in a circle until dough comes together and rolls around the bowl.

4 Turn out dough onto the counter, and knead for 5 minutes or until soft and elastic. If it sticks to your hands, dust with flour.

5 Place dough back in the bowl, cover with plastic wrap, and let rise in a warm, draft-free place for 1 hour or until doubled in size.

6 Punch down dough, knead, shape into a ball, place in the prepared container, and cover tightly with plastic wrap. Allow bread to rise for 35 minutes or until doubled in size.

7 Set the pressure cooker to medium (traditional)/high (electric) heat, and bring to a boil. Add bread in container to the cooker.

8 Lock on the lid, and bring pressure to level 2 (traditional)/high (electric). Reduce heat to low, and cook at 2/high for 20 minutes. Remove from (traditional)/turn off (electric) heat, perform a natural release, and remove the lid.

9 Lift bread out of the cooker, uncover, and shake bread out of the can onto a cooling rack. Cool completely before slicing and serving.

This **tender** and **moist cornbread** goes great with ham and beans, soups, and chilies and makes amazing ham sandwiches.

Cornbread

1 (8-PIECE) LOAF	20 MINUTES	23 MINUTES	2/HIGH

INGREDIENTS

2 cups yellow cornmeal

⅓ cup all-purpose flour

1 tsp. kosher salt

½ tsp. baking soda

½ tsp. baking powder

1 TB. sugar

1½ cups buttermilk

2 large eggs

METHOD

1 Add a trivet to a 6-quart (5.5l) pressure cooker, and fill with the minimum amount of water allowed for your cooker. Butter an 8-inch (20cm) cake pan with 2-inch (5cm) sides and a piece of aluminum foil large enough to cover the pan.

2 In a large bowl, and using a wooden spoon, combine yellow cornmeal, all-purpose flour, kosher salt, baking soda, baking powder, and sugar. Add buttermilk and eggs, and mix until smooth. Pour batter into the prepared cake pan, cover with buttered foil (butter side down), and crimp edges tightly.

3 Fold a long piece of foil lengthwise into a 2-inch (5cm) belt, tuck under the pan, and use the loose ends to lower the pan into the cooker. Set heat to medium (traditional)/high (electric), and bring to a boil.

4 Lock on the lid, bring pressure to level 2 (traditional)/high (electric), and cook for 23 minutes. Remove from (traditional)/turn off (electric) heat, perform a natural release, and remove the lid.

5 Lift cake pan out of the cooker, cut bread cut into 8 pieces, and serve with lots of butter.

NUTRITION PER SERVING

Calories: 220	Sugars: 4g	Protein: 6g	Cholesterol: 60mg
Carbohydrates: 39g	Dietary fiber: 1g	Fat: 3g	Sodium: 310mg

desserts

Custards, cheesecakes, fruit, and more cook to perfection under pressure for delicate desserts that will leave friends and family begging for your recipes.

These **lovely lemon pots,** like crust-free lemon bars but creamier, are **tart** and refreshing.

Lemon Pots de Crème

🍴 5 (4-OUNCE; 120ML) POTS	🥄 20 MINUTES + COOL TIME	🔥 10 MINUTES	⏱ 2/HIGH

INGREDIENTS

1½ cups heavy cream

⅓ cup sugar

1 tsp. lemon zest

4 large egg yolks

Juice of 2 large lemons (¼ cup)

METHOD

1 Add a trivet and steamer basket to a 6-quart (5.5l) pressure cooker, and fill with the minimum amount of water allowed for your cooker.

2 In a small saucepan over medium heat, combine heavy cream, sugar, and lemon zest. Bring to a simmer, stir for 2 minutes or until sugar is dissolved, and remove from heat.

3 In a medium bowl, whisk egg yolks until smooth.

4 While whisking, drizzle 1 cup hot cream into yolks. Keep whisking so heat of cream tempers but doesn't cook eggs. Continue to drizzle in rest of cream, and add lemon juice.

5 Strain mixture into a 3-cup or larger measuring cup to remove lemon zest.

6 Pour 4 ounces (120ml) mixture each into 5 (6-ounce; 175ml) ramekins. Cover ramekins tightly with aluminum foil, and place in the steamer basket, stacking in a pyramid if necessary to fit. Set heat to medium (traditional)/high (electric), and bring to a boil.

7 Lock on the lid, bring pressure to level 2 (traditional)/high (electric), and cook for 10 minutes. Turn off heat, and let the ramekins sit for 10 minutes. Remove the lid.

8 Lift out one ramekin, and remove the foil, being careful not to let any water fall on surface of crème. Gently shake ramekin. Crème should be firm; if it jiggles, re-cover, return to the cooker, lock on the lid, and cook at level 2/high for 5 minutes.

9 Transfer ramekins to a baking sheet, remove the foil, and refrigerate for 1 hour. Cover crème with plastic wrap or foil so it doesn't form a skin, and chill for at least 2 hours or overnight. Serve cold.

NUTRITION PER SERVING

Calories: 340

Carbohydrates: 13g

Sugars: 10g

Dietary fiber: 0g

Protein: 4g

Fat: 31g

Cholesterol: 310mg

Sodium: 35mg

This **luscious custardlike dessert** is reminiscent of a **creamy, smooth** brownie. It's **rich** and **decadent.**

Chocolate Pots de Crème

🍴 4 (5-OUNCE; 150ML) POTS	🥄 30 MINUTES + COOL TIME	🔥 10 MINUTES	⏲ 2/HIGH

INGREDIENTS

- 3 large egg yolks
- ¾ cup heavy cream
- ¾ cup whole milk
- 1½ TB. sugar
- 4 oz. (110g) 72 percent dark chocolate

METHOD

1 Add a trivet and steamer basket to a 6-quart (5.5l) pressure cooker, and fill with the minimum amount of water allowed for your cooker.

2 In a medium bowl, whisk egg yolks until smooth.

3 In a small saucepan over medium heat, combine heavy cream, whole milk, sugar, and dark chocolate. Bring to a simmer, and stir for 2 minutes or until sugar is dissolved, chocolate is melted, and liquid begins to bubble at the edges of the pan. Remove from heat.

4 While whisking, add ½ cup hot chocolate to eggs. Keep whisking so heat of chocolate tempers but doesn't cook eggs. Continue to add rest of chocolate.

5 Divide mixture among 4 (6-ounce; 175ml) ramekins. Cover each ramekin tightly with aluminum foil, and place in the steamer basket, stacking in a pyramid if necessary to fit. Set heat to medium (traditional)/high (electric), and bring to a boil.

6 Lock on the lid, bring pressure to level 2 (traditional)/high (electric), and cook for 10 minutes. Turn off heat, and let the ramekins sit for 10 minutes. Remove the lid.

7 Lift out one ramekin, and remove the foil, being careful not to let any water fall on surface of crème. Gently shake ramekin. Crème should be firm; if it jiggles, re-cover, return to the cooker, lock on the lid, and cook at level 2/high for 5 minutes.

8 Transfer ramekins to a baking sheet, remove the foil, and refrigerate for 1 hour. Cover crème with plastic wrap or foil so it doesn't form a skin, and chill for at least 2 hours or overnight. Serve cold, plain, with whipped cream, or with raspberries.

NUTRITION PER SERVING

Calories: 390
Carbohydrates: 26g
Sugars: 15g
Dietary fiber: 2g
Protein: 6g
Fat: 31g
Cholesterol: 330mg
Sodium: 50mg

This **sweet, maple syrup custard** dessert is topped with a decadent **brown sugar caramel sauce.**

Maple Cream **Caramels**

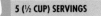

🍴 5 (½ CUP) SERVINGS	🍲 30 MINUTES + COOL TIME	🔥 20 MINUTES	⏲ 2/HIGH

INGREDIENTS

4 large egg yolks

⅓ cup granulated sugar

⅓ cup brown sugar, firmly packed

¼ cup water

2 cups heavy cream

½ cup pure maple syrup

NUTRITION PER SERVING

Calories: **560**

Carbohydrates: **44g**

Sugars: **40g**

Dietary fiber: **0g**

Protein: **6g**

Fat: **42g**

Cholesterol: **410mg**

Sodium: **50mg**

METHOD

1 Add a trivet and steamer basket to a 6-quart (5.5l) pressure cooker, and add 2 cups water.

2 In a medium bowl, whisk egg yolks until smooth.

3 In a small saucepan over medium heat, combine granulated sugar, brown sugar, and water, and cook, without stirring, until amber at edges. Gently swirl or stir with a clean wooden spoon, and cook until caramel is dark amber. Immediately divide into 5 (4-ounce; 110g) ramekins, and let harden for at least 10 minutes.

4 Carefully wash out hot saucepan. Add heavy cream and maple syrup, return to medium heat, and bring to a hard simmer. Remove from heat.

5 While whisking, slowly drizzle ½ cup hot cream into yolks. Keep whisking so heat of cream tempers but doesn't cook eggs. Continue to drizzle in rest of cream.

6 Divide custard mixture among ramekins, cover each ramekin tightly with aluminum foil, and place in the steamer basket, stacking ramekins in a pyramid if necessary to fit. Set heat to high (traditional)/high (electric), and bring to a boil.

7 Lock on the lid, and bring pressure to level 2 (traditional)/high (electric). Reduce heat to low, and cook at 2/high for 20 minutes. Turn off heat, and let caramels sit for 20 minutes. Remove the lid.

8 Transfer ramekins to a cooling rack, and gently remove the foil, being careful not to let any water fall on surface of caramels. Refrigerate overnight.

9 Run a thin-blade knife around the edge of ramekins, and invert onto a plate. Spread a kitchen towel on the counter, and sharply tap plate onto the towel to release custard from the ramekin. Serve cold.

Cracking a spoon through the **burnt sugar topping** of a good **crème brûlée**, exposing the **rich vanilla cream** underneath, is a treat in itself.

Crème **Brûlée**

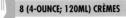

8 (4-OUNCE; 120ML) CRÈMES	15 MINUTES + COOL TIME	15 MINUTES	2/HIGH

INGREDIENTS

1 qt. (1l) heavy cream

1 tsp. vanilla paste, vanilla extract, or seeds from 1 vanilla pod

4 large egg yolks

¾ cup sugar

METHOD

1 Add a trivet and steamer basket to a 6-quart (5.5l) pressure cooker, and fill with the minimum amount of water allowed for your cooker.

2 In a medium saucepan over medium-high heat, bring heavy cream to a simmer.

3 In a large bowl, whisk together vanilla paste, egg yolks, and ½ cup sugar.

4 While whisking, drizzle 1 cup hot cream into egg mixture. Keep whisking so heat of cream tempers but doesn't cook eggs. Continue to drizzle in rest of cream. Skim off any foam on top of crème brûlée.

5 Pour 4 ounces (120ml) mixture each into 8 (6-ounce; 175ml) ramekins. Cover each ramekin tightly with aluminum foil, and place in the steamer basket, stacking ramekins in a pyramid if necessary to fit. Set heat to medium-high (traditional)/high (electric), and bring to a boil.

6 Lock on the lid, and bring pressure to level 2 (traditional)/high (electric). Reduce heat to low, and cook at 2/high for 15 minutes. Turn off heat, and let crème brûlées sit for 10 minutes. Remove the lid.

7 Lift out a ramekin, and remove the foil, being careful not to let any water fall on crème brûlée. Gently shake ramekin. Crème brûlée should be firm; if it jiggles, re-cover, return to the cooker, lock on the lid, and cook at level 2/high for 10 minutes.

8 Transfer ramekins to a baking sheet, remove the foil, and refrigerate for at least 3 hours. If refrigerating overnight, cover crème brûlée with plastic wrap or foil so it doesn't form a skin.

9 To serve, spoon 2 teaspoons sugar on top of each crème brûlée, and gently shake to distribute. Using a kitchen torch or oven broiler, brown sugar. Serve immediately.

NUTRITION PER SERVING

Calories: **500**

Carbohydrates: **17g**

Sugars: **14g**

Dietary fiber: **0g**

Protein: **5g**

Fat: **48g**

Cholesterol: **340mg**

Sodium: **50mg**

Your pressure cooker excels at making flan. The **custard** finishes with a **smooth texture**, a **lovely vanilla note,** and a deep **caramel-coffee flavor.**

Caribbean-Style **Flan**

| 🍴 1 (8-INCH; 20CM) FLAN | 🕑 30 MINUTES + COOL TIME | 🔥 20 MINUTES | ⏲ 2/HIGH |

INGREDIENTS

- 1¼ cups sugar
- ¼ cup water
- 1 (14-oz.; 400g) can sweetened, condensed milk
- 2 cups whole milk
- 3 large eggs
- 2 tsp. vanilla paste, vanilla extract, or seeds from 1 vanilla pod
- ⅛ tsp. kosher salt

NUTRITION PER SERVING

Calories: **300**
Carbohydrates: **55g**
Sugars: **55g**
Dietary fiber: **0g**
Protein: **8g**
Fat: **7g**
Cholesterol: **100mg**
Sodium: **140mg**

METHOD

1 Add a trivet to the bottom of a 6-quart (5.5l) pressure cooker. Add 2 cups water.

2 In a medium saucepan over medium-high heat, combine sugar and water, and cook, without stirring, until amber at edges. Gently swirl, and cook until caramel is dark amber.

3 Immediately pour caramel into an 8-inch (20cm) cake pan, and quickly but gently swirl pan to coat bottom with caramel. Set aside for at least 10 minutes.

4 In a large bowl, whisk together condensed milk, whole milk, eggs, vanilla paste, and kosher salt. Using a fine mesh strainer, strain custard into cake pan to remove any undissolved egg whites. Cover the pan tightly with aluminum foil.

5 Fold a long piece of foil lengthwise into a 2-inch (5cm) belt, tuck under the pan, and use the loose ends to lower the pan into the cooker. Set heat to medium-high (traditional)/high (electric), and bring to a boil.

6 Lock on the lid, and bring pressure to level 2 (traditional)/high (electric). Reduce heat to low, and cook at 2/high for 20 minutes. Turn off heat, and let flan sit for 20 minutes. Remove the lid.

7 Lift out cake pan, and remove the foil, being careful not to let any water fall on surface of flan. Gently shake pan. Flan should be firm; if it jiggles, re-cover, return to the cooker, lock on the lid, and cook at level 2/high for 10 minutes.

8 Refrigerate for 1 hour. Cover flan with plastic wrap or foil so it doesn't form a skin, and chill for at least 2 hours or overnight.

9 Run a thin-blade knife around the edge of the cake pan. Place a large plate with a lip (at least 2 inches; 5cm larger than flan to catch caramel) top down on the pan, invert the pan and plate to release flan, gently tapping the bottom of the pan if necessary, and lift off pan. Cut into 8 pieces, and serve.

This **cheesecake** is so versatile. Serve it topped with **blueberries, cherries, or raspberries**—or all three. It's also delicious plain.

Classic **Cheesecake**

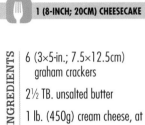

| 1 (8-INCH; 20CM) CHEESECAKE | 30 MINUTES + COOL TIME | 35 MINUTES | 2/HIGH |

INGREDIENTS

- 6 (3×5-in.; 7.5×12.5cm) graham crackers
- 2½ TB. unsalted butter
- 1 lb. (450g) cream cheese, at room temperature
- 1 tsp. vanilla paste, or 1½ tsp. vanilla extract
- ½ cup sugar
- ¼ tsp. kosher salt
- 2 large eggs, at room temperature
- ½ cup sour cream, at room temperature

NUTRITION PER SERVING

Calories: **420**

Carbohydrates: **19g**

Sugars: **16g**

Dietary fiber: **0g**

Protein: **7g**

Fat: **36g**

Cholesterol: **180mg**

Sodium: **390mg**

METHOD

1 Add a trivet to the bottom of a 6-quart (5.5l) pressure cooker. Be sure an 8-inch (20cm) springform pan will fit inside with at least ¾ inch (2cm) space at the edges. Add enough water to reach the bottom of the trivet. Butter an 8-inch (20cm) springform pan with 1 teaspoon unsalted butter.

2 In a food processor fitted with a metal chopping blade, pulse graham crackers and unsalted butter to a crumb consistency. Transfer to the pan, and press into an even layer.

3 In a large bowl, and using an electric mixer on medium, beat cream cheese for 2 minutes or until smooth. Scrape down the sides of the bowl, and beat again. Add vanilla paste, sugar, kosher salt, eggs, and sour cream, and beat until smooth. Pour filling into crust, and smooth to an even layer. Cover the pan tightly with aluminum foil, and secure with string or a rubber band.

4 Fold a long piece of foil lengthwise into a 2-inch (5cm) belt, tuck under the pan, and use the loose ends to lower the pan into the cooker. Set heat to high (traditional)/high (electric), and bring to a boil.

5 Lock on the lid, bring pressure to level 2 (traditional)/high (electric), and cook for 35 minutes. Turn off heat, and let cheesecake sit for 20 minutes. Remove the lid.

6 Lift out the pan to a cooling rack, and remove the foil, being careful not to let any water fall on surface of cheesecake. Let cheesecake cool for 30 minutes, and refrigerate overnight.

7 Run a thin-blade knife around the edge of the pan, and remove the springform ring. Cut cheesecake into 6 pieces, and serve.

1 (9-INCH; 23CM) CHEESECAKE | 1 HOUR + REST/CHILL TIME | 40 MINUTES | 2/HIGH

INGREDIENTS

12 (3×5-in.; 7.5×12.5cm) chocolate graham crackers

2 tsp. plus 1 TB. cocoa powder

¼ cup plus ⅓ cup unsalted butter

1¾ cups sugar

⅓ cup water

¾ cup heavy cream

½ tsp. vanilla extract

4 oz. (110g) dark chocolate, plus more for garnish

2 (8-oz.; 225g) pkg. cream cheese, at room temperature

2 large eggs, at room temperature

¼ cup sour cream, at room temperature

½ cup pecans, chopped

NUTRITION PER SERVING

Calories: 880
Carbohydrates: 67g
Sugars: 55g
Dietary fiber: 3g
Protein: 9g
Fat: 70g
Cholesterol: 250mg
Sodium: 320mg

METHOD

1 Add a trivet to the bottom of a 6-quart (5.5l) pressure cooker. Add enough water to reach the bottom of the trivet.

2 In a food processor fitted with a metal chopping blade, pulse chocolate graham crackers, 2 teaspoons cocoa powder, and ¼ cup unsalted butter to a crumb consistency. Transfer to a 9-inch (23cm) springform pan, and press into an even layer.

3 In a medium saucepan over medium-high heat, combine 1¼ cups sugar and water, and cook, without stirring, until amber at edges. Gently swirl, and cook until caramel is dark amber.

4 Drizzle in heavy cream while stirring, and stir in remaining ⅓ cup unsalted butter and vanilla extract. Remove from heat.

5 In a small saucepan over very low heat, melt dark chocolate.

6 In a medium bowl, and using an electric mixer on medium, beat cream cheese for 2 minutes or until it follows the beaters in ribbons. Add eggs, sour cream, melted chocolate, remaining ½ cup sugar, and remaining 1 tablespoon cocoa powder, and beat until smooth. Pour into crust, and smooth to the edges of the pan. Cover the pan tightly with aluminum foil, and secure foil with string or a rubber band.

7 Fold a long piece of foil lengthwise into a 2-inch (5cm) belt, tuck under the pan, and use the loose ends to lower the pan into the cooker. Set heat to medium-high (traditional)/high (electric), and bring to a boil.

8 Lock on the lid, bring pressure to level 2 (traditional)/high (electric), and cook for 40 minutes. Remove from (traditional)/turn off (electric) heat, and let cake sit for 20 minutes. Remove the lid.

9 Lift out cake pan, uncover, and gently shake. Cake should be firm; if it jiggles, re-cover, return to the cooker, lock on the lid, and cook at level 2/high for 10 minutes.

10 Refrigerate cake for at least 3 hours.

11 Pour caramel over cake to form an ⅛-inch (3mm) thick circle that stops just short of the edges, and sprinkle with pecans. Cover with plastic wrap, and refrigerate for 4 hours or overnight.

12 Run a thin-blade knife around edges of the pan, and remove the springform ring. Grate dark chocolate over top of cheesecake, cut into 8 pieces, and serve.

This **delectable** dessert is for **chocolate lovers.** And **cheesecake lovers.** And caramel lovers.

Chocolate Caramel **Cheesecake**

Rice pudding is a **homey dessert.** This version is prepared with **traditional flavors,** but you can omit these spices and customize as you like.

Rice **Pudding**

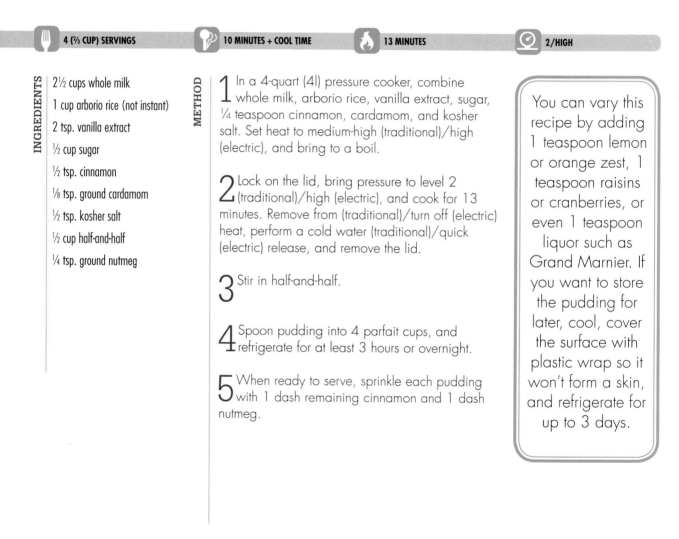

4 (⅔ CUP) SERVINGS   10 MINUTES + COOL TIME   13 MINUTES   2/HIGH

INGREDIENTS

2½ cups whole milk

1 cup arborio rice (not instant)

2 tsp. vanilla extract

½ cup sugar

½ tsp. cinnamon

⅛ tsp. ground cardamom

½ tsp. kosher salt

½ cup half-and-half

¼ tsp. ground nutmeg

METHOD

1 In a 4-quart (4l) pressure cooker, combine whole milk, arborio rice, vanilla extract, sugar, ¼ teaspoon cinnamon, cardamom, and kosher salt. Set heat to medium-high (traditional)/high (electric), and bring to a boil.

2 Lock on the lid, bring pressure to level 2 (traditional)/high (electric), and cook for 13 minutes. Remove from (traditional)/turn off (electric) heat, perform a cold water (traditional)/quick (electric) release, and remove the lid.

3 Stir in half-and-half.

4 Spoon pudding into 4 parfait cups, and refrigerate for at least 3 hours or overnight.

5 When ready to serve, sprinkle each pudding with 1 dash remaining cinnamon and 1 dash nutmeg.

You can vary this recipe by adding 1 teaspoon lemon or orange zest, 1 teaspoon raisins or cranberries, or even 1 teaspoon liquor such as Grand Marnier. If you want to store the pudding for later, cool, cover the surface with plastic wrap so it won't form a skin, and refrigerate for up to 3 days.

NUTRITION PER SERVING

Calories: 370	Sugars: 26g	Protein: 9g	Cholesterol: 25mg
Carbohydrates: 66g	Dietary fiber: 1g	Fat: 9g	Sodium: 320mg

Rich with **warm spices** and a **tender, melt-in-your-mouth pudding,** this **creamy** dessert is a welcome addition to family and holiday dinners.

Bread Pudding with
Whiskey Sauce

 8 (⅔ CUP) SERVINGS   20 MINUTES + COOL TIME   25 MINUTES   2/HIGH

INGREDIENTS

- 6 large egg yolks
- ½ cup plus ⅓ cup sugar
- 3 cups whole milk
- 1 tsp. orange zest
- 1 tsp. vanilla extract
- ½ tsp. cinnamon
- ¼ tsp. ground nutmeg
- 6 slices white bread, cut into ½-in. (2.5cm) cubes (2 cups)
- ⅓ cup raisins
- ⅓ cup whiskey
- 3 tsp. unsalted butter
- 2 TB. heavy cream

NUTRITION PER SERVING

Calories: **270**
Carbohydrates: **30g**
Sugars: **25g**
Dietary fiber: **1g**
Protein: **7g**
Fat: **12g**
Cholesterol: **280mg**
Sodium: **115mg**

METHOD

1 Add a trivet to the bottom of a 6-quart (5.5l) pressure cooker. Add 2 cups water. Butter an 8-inch (20cm) cake pan and a piece of aluminum foil large enough to cover it.

2 In a large bowl, whisk together 3 egg yolks and ½ cup sugar. Whisk in whole milk, orange zest, vanilla extract, cinnamon, and nutmeg.

3 Add bread to the cake pan, and spread evenly. Sprinkle on raisins, pour in pudding, and push down any floating bread. Cover the pan with buttered foil (butter side down), and tightly crimp on the pan. Place the cake pan in the cooker, and let sit for 20 minutes.

4 Set heat to medium-high (traditional)/high (electric), and bring to a boil.

5 Lock on the lid, and bring pressure to level 2 (traditional)/high (electric). Reduce heat to low, and cook at 2/high for 25 minutes. Turn off heat, and let pudding sit for 20 minutes. Remove the lid.

6 In a small mixing bowl, whisk together remaining ⅓ cup sugar and remaining 3 egg yolks.

7 In a small saucepan over medium heat, whisk together whiskey and unsalted butter. Bring to a boil, remove from heat, and slowly whisk whiskey mixture into eggs. Whisk in heavy cream. Return sauce to the saucepan, set heat to low, and cook, stirring, for 1 minute or until sauce begins to thicken. Remove from heat.

8 Lift cake pan out of the pressure cooker, and remove the foil. Cool for 1 hour.

9 Scoop out pudding into individual bowls, and serve with whiskey sauce on the side.

6 (5-OUNCE; 150ML) SERVINGS | **30 MINUTES + COOL TIME** | **15 MINUTES** | **2/HIGH**

INGREDIENTS

½ cup small-pearl tapioca

½ cup granulated sugar

2½ cups whole milk

¼ tsp. kosher salt

1½ tsp. vanilla paste, or vanilla extract

½ cup heavy cream, very cold

1 TB. confectioners' sugar

¼ cup crumbled English toffee

> Be careful when caramelizing the sugar. It gets very, very hot and can burn you easily.

METHOD

1 Place tapioca in a strainer, rinse under cold water, and set aside.

2 In a 4-quart (4l) pressure cooker set to medium (traditional)/high (electric) heat, add granulated sugar and shake the cooker to evenly distribute sugar. Cook, watching sugar closely, until it begins to caramelize at the edges and darken as it melts. Using a clean wooden spoon, stir sugar. It'll clump and melt, but in the end, it'll be an amber to brown-colored liquid.

3 In a small saucepan over medium heat, warm whole milk until just short of boiling.

4 While stirring, drizzle 2 cups hot milk into sugar. Don't worry if sugar clumps; it'll melt.

5 Add tapioca, kosher salt, and 1 teaspoon vanilla paste, and stir until sugar dissolves and milk begins to boil.

6 Lock on the lid, and bring pressure to level 2 (traditional)/high (electric). Reduce heat to low, and cook for 15 minutes. Remove from (traditional)/turn off (electric) heat, and let pudding sit for 10 minutes. Perform a natural release, and remove the lid.

7 Add remaining ½ cup hot milk, return to medium-low (traditional)/low (electric) heat, and whisk until tapioca is loose and not clumping. (This might take a little while, so be patient.)

8 Ladle tapioca into small containers, and let it cool for 1 hour. When it's warm but not hot, cover tapioca with plastic wrap, and refrigerate for at least 3 hours or until set.

9 When ready to serve, in a medium bowl, whisk very cold heavy cream, remaining ½ teaspoon vanilla paste, and confectioners' sugar until stiff peaks form.

10 Uncover pudding, top with whipped cream, sprinkle with English toffee, and serve.

NUTRITION PER SERVING

Calories: **270**

Carbohydrates: **36g**

Sugars: **25g**

Dietary fiber: **0g**

Protein: **4g**

Fat: **14g**

Cholesterol: **40mg**

Sodium: **170mg**

Sweet tapioca pudding is a favorite for kids and adults alike. This version is matured a bit with **caramel** and **vanilla** flavors.

Caramel Vanilla **Tapioca Pudding**

This **traditional British holiday** dessert is a wonderful addition to family dinners. Conventional versions are often heavy; this is **lighter.**

Christmas **Pudding**

| 🍴 1 (1½ QUART; 1.5l) PUDDING | 🥄 30 MINUTES | 🔥 1 HOUR | ⏲ 2/HIGH |

INGREDIENTS

1¾ cups mixed dried raisins, chopped prunes, cherries, cranberries, and apricots

½ cup dried dates, pitted and chopped

2 TB. minced crystallized ginger

1 tsp. orange zest

6 slices fresh white bread, chopped in a food processor to a fine crumb (2½ cups)

3 TB. unsalted butter or vegetable shortening, softened

1¾ cups sugar

1 cup walnuts, chopped

1 large egg

⅔ cup whole milk

⅓ cup water

¾ cup heavy cream

⅓ cup unsalted butter

½ tsp. vanilla extract

METHOD

1 Add a trivet to the bottom of a 6-quart (5.5l) pressure cooker. Add enough water to reach the bottom of the trivet. Grease a 1½-quart (1.5l) heat-proof pudding mold with unsalted butter.

2 In a large bowl, combine fruit, dates, crystallized ginger, orange zest, breadcrumbs, softened unsalted butter, ½ cup sugar, walnuts, egg, and whole milk.

3 Transfer to the mold, and gently pack. Cover with aluminum foil, and secure foil with string or a rubber band. Place the mold in the pressure cooker, set heat to high (traditional)/ high (electric), and bring to a boil.

4 Lock on the lid, and bring pressure to level 2 (traditional)/high (electric). Reduce heat to low, and cook at 2/high for 1 hour. Turn off heat, and let pudding sit for 20 minutes. Perform a natural release, and remove the lid.

5 Remove the mold from the cooker, and invert pudding onto a platter.

6 In a medium saucepan over medium-high heat, combine remaining 1¼ cups sugar and water, and cook, without stirring, until amber at edges. Gently swirl or stir with a clean wooden spoon, and cook until caramel is dark amber.

7 Drizzle in heavy cream while stirring. Stir in unsalted butter and vanilla extract, and remove from heat.

8 Top pudding with caramel sauce, and serve with whipped cream.

NUTRITION PER SERVING

| Calories: **490** | Sugars: **56g** | Protein: **6g** | Cholesterol: **55mg** |
| Carbohydrates: **82g** | Dietary fiber: **3g** | Fat: **18g** | Sodium: **220mg** |

This easy recipe yields a **wonderful caramel concoction** with a **sweet flavor.** It's a perfect **dip for apple slices, ice cream topping,** or **jelly roll cake filling.**

Dulce **de Leche**

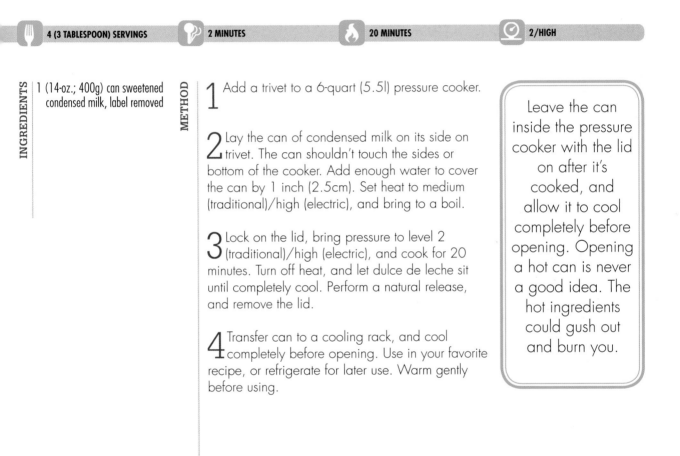

| 4 (3 TABLESPOON) SERVINGS | 2 MINUTES | 20 MINUTES | 2/HIGH |

INGREDIENTS

1 (14-oz.; 400g) can sweetened condensed milk, label removed

METHOD

1 Add a trivet to a 6-quart (5.5l) pressure cooker.

2 Lay the can of condensed milk on its side on trivet. The can shouldn't touch the sides or bottom of the cooker. Add enough water to cover the can by 1 inch (2.5cm). Set heat to medium (traditional)/high (electric), and bring to a boil.

3 Lock on the lid, bring pressure to level 2 (traditional)/high (electric), and cook for 20 minutes. Turn off heat, and let dulce de leche sit until completely cool. Perform a natural release, and remove the lid.

4 Transfer can to a cooling rack, and cool completely before opening. Use in your favorite recipe, or refrigerate for later use. Warm gently before using.

Leave the can inside the pressure cooker with the lid on after it's cooked, and allow it to cool completely before opening. Opening a hot can is never a good idea. The hot ingredients could gush out and burn you.

NUTRITION PER SERVING

| Calories: **298** | Sugars: **57g** | Protein: **7.5g** | Cholesterol: **12mg** |
| Carbohydrates: **57g** | Dietary fiber: **0g** | Fat: **4g** | Sodium: **99mg** |

This **delicious, moist** cake is loaded with **gingerbread** flavor. The **vanilla glaze** provides an elegant finish.

Gingerbread Cake with
Vanilla Glaze

1 (8-INCH; 20CM) CAKE   **30 MINUTES**   **25 MINUTES**   **2/HIGH**

INGREDIENTS

½ cup unsalted butter

½ cup granulated sugar

½ cup molasses

¼ cup water

1½ tsp. ground ginger

¾ tsp. cinnamon

¼ tsp. ground cloves

1¼ cups unbleached cake flour

1¼ tsp. baking soda

½ tsp. kosher salt

1 large egg, lightly beaten

3 TB. heavy cream

½ tsp. vanilla extract

¾ cup confectioners' sugar

METHOD

1. Add a trivet to a 6-quart (5.5l) pressure cooker. Add 2 cups water. Butter an 8-inch (20cm) cake pan, and lightly coat bottom and sides with 1 tablespoon flour. Gently tap out excess flour.

2. In a small saucepan over medium heat, combine unsalted butter, granulated sugar, molasses, and water. Cook, stirring, for 2 minutes or until sugar is dissolved and butter is melted. Remove from heat, and set aside to cool.

3. In a large bowl, combine ginger, cinnamon, cloves, cake flour, baking soda, and kosher salt.

4. Add cooled molasses mixture to dry ingredients, add egg, and stir with a heavy-duty wooden spoon until smooth and combined. Scrape batter into the prepared pan, and tap the pan gently to distribute batter. Cover the pan tightly with aluminum foil.

5. Add the cake pan to the pressure cooker, set heat to medium-high (traditional)/high (electric), and bring to a boil.

6. Lock on the lid, and bring pressure to level 2 (traditional)/high (electric). Reduce heat to low, and cook at 2/high for 25 minutes. Remove from (traditional)/turn off (electric) heat, perform a natural release, and remove the lid.

7. Remove the cake pan, uncover, and let cake cool completely on a cooling rack.

8. In a large bowl, whisk heavy cream, vanilla extract, and confectioners' sugar until smooth. Glaze should be runny but not overly so. Add more confectioners' sugar to thicken if necessary. Add more cream, 1 teaspoon at a time, if glaze is too stiff.

9. Run a thin-blade knife around the edge of the cake pan, place a large plate top down on the pan, and invert the pan and plate. Gently tap the bottom of the pan to release cake, and lift off cake pan. Drizzle glaze over top of cake, slice, and serve.

NUTRITION PER SERVING

| Calories: **430** | Sugars: **41g** | Protein: **3g** | Cholesterol: **85mg** |
| Carbohydrates: **64g** | Dietary fiber: **0g** | Fat: **19g** | Sodium: **480mg** |

This cake is a little **gooey,** a little **boozy,** and a little **tart,** thanks to the apples. Don't forget the cardamom. It makes the cake taste like an **apple Danish.**

Rum Raisin, Apple, and Prune **Cake**

| 1 (8-INCH; 20CM) CAKE | 30 MINUTES | 25 MINUTES | 2/HIGH |

INGREDIENTS

2 TB. plus 2 tsp. brown sugar

10 TB. unsalted butter

2 small Fuji apples, peeled and cut into thin half-moons

1½ cups cake flour

1½ tsp. baking powder

⅛ tsp. ground cardamom

1 cup granulated sugar

3 large eggs

¼ cup whole milk

1¼ tsp. vanilla extract

½ cup raisins, soaked in 3 TB. spiced rum for 1 hour

½ cup prunes

½ cup sour cream

NUTRITION PER SERVING

Calories: 440

Carbohydrates: 60g

Sugars: 39g

Dietary fiber: 3g

Protein: 5g

Fat: 19g

Cholesterol: 130mg

Sodium: 140mg

METHOD

1 Add a trivet to a 6-quart (5.5l) pressure cooker. Add 2 cups water. Butter a large piece of aluminum foil.

2 In a small bowl, cream 2 tablespoons brown sugar and 2 tablespoons unsalted butter. Spread in the bottom of an 8-inch (20cm) cake pan, and layer Fuji apple slices on top.

3 In a medium bowl, combine cake flour, baking powder, and cardamom.

4 In a large bowl, cream granulated sugar and remaining 8 table-spoons unsalted butter until smooth. Add eggs, whole milk, and 1 teaspoon vanilla extract, and stir.

5 Combine granulated sugar–egg mixture with dry ingredients, and stir in raisins and prunes. Gently pour batter over apples, and spread to the edge of the pan. Cover with buttered foil (butter side down), and tightly crimp foil to the pan.

6 Fold a long piece of foil lengthwise into a 2-inch (5cm) belt, tuck under the pan, and use the loose ends to lower the pan into the cooker. Set to heat medium (traditional)/high (electric), and bring to a boil.

7 Lock on the lid, bring pressure to level 2 (traditional)/high (electric), and cook for 25 minutes. Turn off heat, let cake sit for 20 minutes, and remove the lid.

8 Lift the pan out of the cooker, and remove the foil. Cool cake on a cooling rack.

9 In a medium bowl, whisk together remaining ¼ teaspoon vanilla extract, remaining 2 teaspoons brown sugar, and sour cream until smooth.

10 Turn out cake, upside down, onto a plate. Cut into 8 pieces, top with brown sugar sour cream, and serve.

Whether spooned over **vanilla ice cream** or served in a bowl with a **drizzle of cream** and a bit of **granola,** this is a wonderful dessert.

Boozy Dried Fruit **Compote**

🍴 8 (½ CUP) SERVINGS	🥄 10 MINUTES	🔥 8 MINUTES	⏱ 1/LOW

INGREDIENTS

1 cup dried apples, chopped into ¾-in. (2cm) pieces

1 cup small prunes

½ cup dried apricots

¼ cup raisins

½ cup dried cranberries

1 cup water

1 cup dry red wine

1 slice lemon

½ cup sugar

1 tsp. vanilla paste, or vanilla extract

1 (3-in.; 7.5cm) cinnamon stick

⅛ tsp. ground nutmeg

1 pinch cardamom

METHOD

1 In a 4-quart (4l) pressure cooker, combine apples, prunes, apricots, raisins, cranberries, water, red wine, lemon slice, sugar, vanilla paste, cinnamon stick, nutmeg, and cardamom. Set heat to medium (traditional)/high (electric), and bring to a boil.

2 Lock on the lid, and bring pressure to level 1 (traditional)/low (electric). Reduce heat to low, and cook at 1/low for 8 minutes. Remove from (traditional)/turn off (electric) heat, perform a cold water (traditional)/quick (electric) release, and remove the lid.

3 Remove cinnamon stick and lemon slice, and let fruit cool before serving. Refrigerate any leftovers in a jar for up to 2 weeks.

NUTRITION PER SERVING

Calories: **170**	Sugars: **35g**	Protein: **1g**	Cholesterol: **0mg**
Carbohydrates: **45g**	Dietary fiber: **4g**	Fat: **0g**	Sodium: **70mg**

You'll impress guests when you serve these **lovely pears** steamed to **tender perfection** and infused with the perfect amount of **spice** and **sweetness**.

Pears Poached in Red Wine

🍴 4 (1 PEAR) SERVINGS	💨 30 MINUTES	🔥 8 MINUTES	⏱ 2/HIGH

INGREDIENTS

¾ cup dry red wine

½ cup water

1 (3-in.; 7.5cm) cinnamon stick

1 tsp. whole black peppercorns

2 slices lemon

¼ tsp. freshly ground nutmeg, plus more for dusting

½ cup sugar

4 medium firm, almost ripe d' Anjou pears, peeled

½ cup heavy cream

1½ tsp. honey

METHOD

1 In a 4-quart (4l) pressure cooker set to medium-high (traditional)/high (electric) heat, combine red wine, water, cinnamon stick, black peppercorns, lemon slices, nutmeg, and sugar. Add d' Anjou pears, stems up, and bring to a boil.

2 Lock on the lid, bring pressure to level 2 (traditional)/high (electric), and cook for 8 minutes. Remove from (traditional)/turn off (electric) heat, perform a cold water (traditional)/quick (electric) release, and remove the lid.

3 In a medium bowl, whisk heavy cream until it begins to thicken. (You aren't whipping cream, just thickening it.) Add honey, and whisk to combine.

4 Using a slotted spoon, gently transfer pears to a platter.

5 Return the pressure cooker to medium/high heat, and cook for 5 minutes or until spiced wine is reduced by half or becomes syrupy.

6 Spoon syrup over pears, dollop with honey cream, and dust with ground nutmeg. Serve with extra syrup on the side.

When spooning the reduced syrup over the cooked pears, avoid getting any peppercorns, lemon slices, or the cinnamon stick in the serving dishes. You can strain the sauce and serve it on the side if you like.

NUTRITION PER SERVING

Calories: 260

Carbohydrates: 35g

Sugars: 20g

Dietary fiber: 0g

Protein: 2g

Fat: 11g

Cholesterol: 40mg

Sodium: 15mg

Appendix

Helpful Tables

This appendix holds some handy tables for quick reference. Use them for a reminder of cook times or to help convert conventional recipes for use in a pressure cooker.

MEATS

MEAT	WEIGHT	LIQUID	COOK TIME	PRESSURE
Chuck roast	3 pounds (1.5kg)	½ cup or more	45 minutes	level 2 (traditional)/ high (electric)
Chuck roast	3 pounds (1.5kg)	½ cup or more	55 minutes (for shredded beef)	level 2 (traditional)/ high (electric)
Pork loin	2 pounds (1kg)	½ cup or more	30 minutes (sliced)	level 2 (traditional)/ high (electric)
Stew meat	2 pounds (1kg)	½ cup or more	20 minutes	level 2 (traditional)/ high (electric)
Whole chicken	2½ to 3 pounds (1.25 to 1.5kg)	½ cup or more	15 to 20 minutes	level 2 (traditional)/ high (electric)

POTATOES

POTATO	AMOUNT/ SIZE	LIQUID (WATER)	COOK TIME	PRESSURE
Baby potatoes	2 ounces (55g)	1 cup	5 or 6 minutes	level 2 (traditional)/ high (electric)
Red potatoes	halved; 6 to 8 ounces (170 to 225g)	1 cup	10 to 12 minutes	level 2 (traditional)/ high (electric)
Red potatoes	whole; 6 to 8 ounces (170 to 225g)	1 cup	18 minutes	level 2 (traditional)/ high (electric)
Russet potatoes	whole; 1 pound (450g)	1 cup	25 to 30 minutes	level 2 (traditional)/ high (electric)
Sweet potatoes	1-inch (2.5cm) cubes	1 cup	5 minutes	level 2 (traditional)/ high (electric)
White potatoes	1-inch (2.5cm) cubes	1 cup	4 minutes	level 2 (traditional)/ high (electric)
Yukon Gold potatoes	whole; 8 ounces (225g)	1 cup	16 minutes	level 2 (traditional)/ high (electric)

All potatoes cook in a steamer basket inside the pressure cooker.

Dried beans cook best if they're presoaked first. For every 1 cup beans, add 4 cups water, and soak for 8 hours or overnight. Discard the soak water, and rinse the beans before cooking. The beans need to be fully hydrated before cooking so they don't absorb all the cooking liquid and scorch.

DRIED BEANS

BEAN	AMOUNT	LIQUID	COOK TIME	PRESSURE
Black beans	1 cup	covered by ½ inch (1.25cm)	10 to 12 minutes	level 2 (traditional)/ high (electric)
Black-eyed peas	1 cup	covered by ½ inch (1.25cm)	8 to 10 minutes	level 2 (traditional)/ high (electric)
Cannellini beans	1 cup	covered by ½ inch (1.25cm)	6 to 8 minutes	level 2 (traditional)/ high (electric)
Chickpeas	1 cup	covered by ½ inch (1.25cm)	10 to 12 minutes	level 2 (traditional)/ high (electric)
du Puy lentils	1 cup	covered by 2 inches (5cm)	6 to 8 minutes	level 1 (traditional)/ low (electric)
Navy beans	1 cup	covered by ½ inch (1.25cm)	6 to 8 minutes	level 2 (traditional)/ high (electric)
Pinto beans	1 cup	covered by ½ inch (1.25cm)	10 to 12 minutes	level 2 (traditional)/ high (electric)
Red kidney beans	1 cup	covered by ½ inch (1.25cm)	10 to 12 minutes	level 2 (traditional)/ high (electric)

All cook times are for beans soaked overnight. In general, lentils and black-eyed peas don't require an overnight soak.

GRAINS AND SEEDS

GRAIN/ SEED	AMOUNT	LIQUID	COOK TIME	PRESSURE
Brown long-grain rice	1 cup	1½ cups	20 to 22 minutes	level 2 (traditional)/ high (electric)
Farro	1 cup	3 cups	15 minutes	level 2 (traditional)/ high (electric)
Jasmine rice	1 cup	1½ cups	5 minutes	level 2 (traditional)/ high (electric)
Pearled barley	1 cup	4½ cups	18 minutes	level 2 (traditional)/ high (electric)
Quinoa	1 cup	2 cups	7 minutes	level 2 (traditional)/ high (electric)
Wheat berries	1 cup	3 cups	22 to 25 minutes	level 2 (traditional)/ high (electric)
White long-grain rice	1 cup	1½ cups	5 minutes	level 2 (traditional)/ high (electric)
Whole oat groats	1 cup	2 cups	14 minutes	level 2 (traditional)/ high (electric)

Index

carrots, 22
    Chuck Roast with Horseradish Cream and Carrots, 143
    Glazed Carrots with Braised Lettuce, 117
    Honey-Glazed Carrots, 116
    Indian Carrot and Lentil Soup, 94
    Pot Roast with Fennel and Carrots, 139
casseroles, Sausage, Onion, and Gruyère Breakfast Casserole, 55
celery root, Root Vegetable Stew, 99
cheesecakes
    Chocolate Caramel Cheesecake, 204–205
    Classic Cheesecake, 203
chicken, 24
    Caribbean Chicken Curry, 152–153
    Chicken and Dumplings, 30, 155
    Chicken Cacciatore, 156–157
    Chicken Salad Deluxe, 30, 74
    Chicken Stock, 38
    Chicken with 40 Cloves of Garlic, 159
    Chinese Red Cooked Chicken, 162
    Hungarian Chicken Paprika, 151
    One-Pot Chicken and Sausage Perloo, 154
    preparing, 27
    Pressure Cooker Tacos, 30
    Smothered Chicken, 158
    Thai-Style Green Curry Chicken, 30, 160–161
Chicken and Dumplings, 155
Chicken Cacciatore, 156–157
Chicken Salad Deluxe, 30, 74
Chicken Stock, 38
Chicken with 40 Cloves of Garlic, 159
chickpeas
    Middle Eastern Hummus, 66–67
    Spicy Chickpea Stew with Sour Tomato Curry, 88–89
    Tuna Salad with Chickpeas, 72–73
chilies
    Roasted Corn and Butternut Squash Chili, 84–85
    Texas-Style Chili Con Carne, 103
Chinese Red Cooked Chicken, 162
Chocolate Caramel Cheesecake, 204–205
Chocolate Pots de Crème, 198
chowders
    Farmhouse Corn Chowder, 91
    New England Fish Chowder, 111

Christmas Pudding, 210
Chuck Roast with Horseradish Cream and Carrots, 143
Classic Beef Brisket, 30, 138
Classic Cheesecake, 203
Classic Egg Salad, 75
cleaning your pressure cooker, 17
cold water pressure release method, 18–19
collard greens
    One-Pot Sausage, Potatoes, and Greens, 171
    Southern Collard Greens, 129
compotes, Boozy Dried Fruit Compote, 215
converting conventional recipes for your pressure cooker, 26–27
corn
    Farmhouse Corn Chowder, 91
    Roasted Corn and Butternut Squash Chili, 84–85
Cornbread, 193
Corned Beef, 135
cornmeal, Cornbread, 193
Crème Brûlée, 200–201
Croutons, 95
Crustless Sandwich Bread, 192
Cuban Black Bean Soup with Sherry, 90
Cuban-Style Ropa Vieja, 136–137
Curried Butternut Squash Soup, 96–97
curries
    Fish Curry, 175
    Spicy Chickpea Stew with Sour Tomato Curry, 88–89
    Thai-Style Green Curry Chicken, 160–161

D

desserts, 216–217
    Boozy Dried Fruit Compote, 215
    Bread Pudding with Whiskey Sauce, 207
    Caramel Vanilla Tapioca Pudding, 208–209
    Caribbean-Style Flan, 202
    Chocolate Caramel Cheesecake, 204–205
    Chocolate Pots de Crème, 198
    Christmas Pudding, 210
    Classic Cheesecake, 203
    Crème Brûlée, 200–201
    Dulce de Leche, 211
    Gingerbread Cake with Vanilla Glaze, 212–213

Lemon Pots de Crème, 196–197
    Maple Cream Caramels, 199
    Pears Poached in Red Wine, 216–217
    Rice Pudding, 206
    Rum Raisin, Apple, and Prune Cake, 214
Dirty Oats with Lentils, 184
Dulce de Leche, 211

E

Easy Dried Beans, 43
eggplant, Ratatouille, 114–115
eggs
    Classic Deviled Eggs, 62–63
    Classic Egg Salad, 75
    Egg Cups, 50
    Eggs en Cocotte à la Crème, 48–49
    Pressure Cooker Eggs, 40–41
electric pressure cookers, 15
electric stoves, using two burners, 13

F

Farmhouse Corn Chowder, 91
Farro Tabbouleh, 78–79
fennel
    Pot Roast with Fennel and Carrots, 139
    Root Vegetable Stew, 99
Fish Curry, 175
Five-Grain Oatmeal, 54
flan, Caribbean-Style Flan, 202
flank steak
    Cuban-Style Ropa Vieja, 137
    Texas-Style Chili Con Carne, 103
French Potato and Leek Soup, 92–93
fruit. *See also specific fruits*
    Apple Cinnamon Breakfast Oats, 51
    Boozy Dried Fruit Compote, 215
    Honey, Raisin, and Quinoa Breakfast Risotto, 56–57
    Lemon Pots de Crème, 196–197
    Pears Poached in Red Wine, 216–217
    Rum Raisin, Apple, and Prune Cake, 214
    Steamed Brown Bread with Raisins, 190–191
frying in your pressure cooker, 25

G

Garlicky White Bean and Parmesan Dip, 64
Gingerbread Cake with Vanilla Glaze, 212–213

Photo Credits:

p. 12: Roger Dixon © Dorling Kindersley, Steve Gorton © Dorling Kindersley, Dave King © Dorling Kindersley

p. 13: © Dorling Kindersley, Dave King © Dorling Kindersley, David Munns © Dorling Kindersley

p. 28: Phillip Dowell © Dorling Kindersley, Roger Dixon © Dorling Kindersley, Dave King © Dorling Kindersley

p. 29: Ian O'Leary © Dorling Kindersley, Roger Dixon © Dorling Kindersley, John Wittaker © Dorling Kindersley, Charlotte Tolhurst © Dorling Kindersley